Nelson and Pam Roth take a look at coaching through the lens of the Nehemiah story. Full of practical structures and relevant applications, the The Nehemiah Response Coaching Model™ will be a great help to the church leader who takes a coaching approach to helping others. Nelson and Pam walk the reader step-by-step through a practical coaching process—one that moves us ultimately toward the goal of transformation on a deeper level.

—Dr. Bob Logan,
author of *The Missional Journey*

Nelson Roth has put his thumb on the key ingredient in church change, the ability to see that you need assistance to change a church and that it is a cyclical process. In his The Nehemiah Response Coaching Model™, he shows leaders how to transition their churches to a place of help, reconciliation, and spiritual transformation. I have been personally blessed by Nelson's insights and compassion, and I recommend his ministry as a timely refocusing of the Body of Christ back to meeting human needs that will lead to spiritual transformation.

—Bob Whitesel, DMin, PhD
Professor of Christian Ministry
and Missional Leadership
Wesley Seminary at Indiana
Wesleyan University

Nelson's Nehemiah Response Coaching Model™ is a how-to biblical transition process. The model, integrated with social and behavioral sciences, fits well with the Transtheoretical Model which proposes how we change. What I like about the Nehemiah Response Coaching Model™ is that it goes beyond behavior change to transformation. This book stands out from the rest of the coaching books and models out there by addressing how a crisis can be responded to from a biblical perspective. We all want to believe that those around us are immune from bad things happening. However, the reality is most people will go through one or more major crises during their lifetime. This is an essential read that will help you respond effectively when those times happen.

—Jamie D. Aten, PhD
Founder and Co-director,
Humanitarian Disaster Institute
Department of Psychology at Wheaton College

Nelson and Pam will not allow leaders to settle for the stagnation of the status quo in their lives or ministry. Nehemiah Response: A Coaching Model will stir your heart and cause you to reflect deeply about God's calling on your life and the legacy of your work. Your vision will be enlarged, your skills will be improved, and your ministry will be different as you engage this process of life transformation.

—David Wetzler
ChurchSmart Resources Publisher
Natural Church Development, Trainer/Coach

The purpose of this coaching model is not self-improvement! Rather, it is the transformation of self-awareness so that we can realize a union with God and ultimately with ourselves. The authors illustrate from their own experience that we can achieve real change in our lives and work when a crisis forces us to stop finessing attitudes and behaviors and we get to work on the source from which they come—our character and self-knowledge. These elements are valuable, but hard to get. If we want to broaden self-knowledge and deepen character, it is actually hard work—like mining for a treasure. When you are ready to be such a miner for profound personal change, it is helpful to have the right tool—the Nehemiah Response Coaching Model™.

—Walter W. Sawatzky, CCLC, CHPC, MTC
Leadership Transition Coach
Design Group International
Milwaukee, Wisconsin

Don't just read this book! Engage in and experience coaching and grow as you use the Nehemiah Response Coaching Model™ as a practical and challenging resource. Engage in self-coaching and get involved in coaching others. Thanks, Nelson and Pam.

—J. D. Landis
Good News Fellowship, Retired Overseer

The Nehemiah Response Coaching Model™is a brilliant resource for determining "what's next?" Using their personal stories and the biblical story of Nehemiah, Nelson and Pam provide a clear, simple blueprint for coaching oneself and others. Draw from their wealth of knowledge to effectively move forward on your journey.

—Dr. Don Eisenhauer, PCC
Coaching at End of Life

NEHEMIAH RESPONSE

NEHEMIAH RESPONSE
...a coaching model

Nelson and Pam Roth, PCC
forward by Dr. J. Val Hastings, MCC

Relevant Ministry Publishing
Pass Christian, MS, United States

Scripture is "NIV" and taken from the Holy Bible, New International Version®, Copyright © 1973, 1978, 1984 by International Bible Society. Used by permission of Zondervan Publishing House. All rights reserved.

Second Printing: 2018
ISBN-13: 978-0692114889
ISBN-10: 0692114882

Relevant Ministry Publishing
503 Church Avenue I Pass Christian, MS 39571
United States

www.relevantministry.org

Book design copyright © 2018 by Relevant Ministry Publishing. All rights reserved. Book layout, cover art and design by Kaila McBride.

dedication

To Jesus Christ, the master coach. To our children—Rod, Angie, and Andrea and their families—some of our greatest encouragers. And to the Relevant Ministry team who, like us, are on a journey of discovering how to minister relevantly.

Nelson and Pam Roth
Co-founders of Relevant Ministry Inc.

contents

foreward

Many of today's ministry leaders advocate a coaching approach to ministry. Most are suggesting that a coaching approach is a crucial component of the missional church going forward. Few however actually describe what a coaching approach to ministry looks like. Nelson and Pam Roth have done just that.

This book expertly describes a coaching approach to ministry, while also offering a helpful coaching model. Nelson and Pam weave the stories of Nehemiah and Hurricane Katrina together and offer the reader a robust resource that is filled with practical and proven steps.

The Nehemiah Response Coaching Model™ is profoundly simple and easy to remember. The stages include the following: Incubation, Implementation, Celebration, and Transformation. Don't let its simplicity fool you. The pages of this book are filled with numerous resources that add depth and breadth to this coaching model.

Where does the depth and breadth of this coaching

model and book come from? It comes from two individuals who have lived this book and have walked this approach daily. It has been my pleasure to observe Nelson and Pam as they have put into writing what they have lived.

This book is ideal for the new or established coach that is looking for a solid biblical coaching model, as well as practical insights about developing a coaching approach to ministry. This book is equally valuable for the person or team that is currently stuck and looking to move forward. Not that a book can replace an actual coach; nevertheless, this book can be a significant resource as you coach yourself and others forward.

Dr. J. Val Hastings, MCC
President and Founder, Coaching4Today's
Leaders and Coaching4Clergy

introduction

Have you ever noticed how difficult it can be to move forward when you need to make an important decision about the future? This was definitely true for me after experiencing Hurricane Katrina. There were days, I literally felt overwhelmed and stuck.

When I reread the words of my first book, *Nehemiah Response: How to Make It Through Your Crisis*, I was surprised how many times I wrote in present tense rather than past tense. That's why I'm energized to write this second book along with my wife, Pam, because we have moved forward, and we're excited to share our discoveries.

Not long after the release of *Nehemiah Response: How to Make It Through Your Crisis*, I discovered the benefits of the coaching approach in my life and the value coaching has to offer to others. While spending time with my mentor coach, J. Val Hastings, I was challenged by him to look at the biblical principles I had written about in Nehemiah Response through the eyes of a coach. "How could I repurpose the book for coaching?" Out of his challenge, the Nehemiah Response Coaching Model™ was birthed. With a fresh look at Nehemiah's biblical principles, a seismic shift was created, which gave me clarity and helped me to move forward.

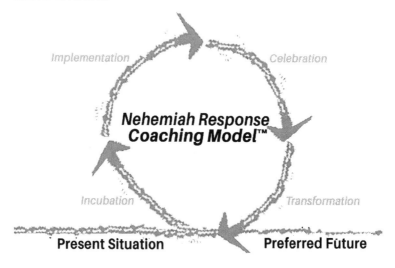

Nehemiah Response: A Coaching Model is written as a coaching approach for anyone to learn the skill of self-coaching and for professional coaches to take coaching to a whole new level.

Whether it is developing steps for your next venture or processing a decision you need to make today, the four stages of the Nehemiah Response Coaching Model™ will help you get from your present situation to your preferred future. So, let's get started!

PART 1

incubation stage

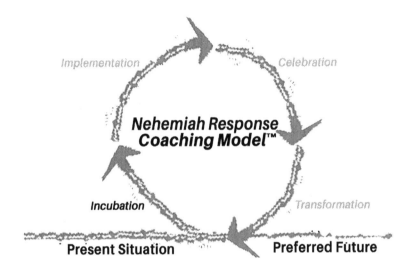

Implementation   Celebration

Nehemiah Response Coaching Model™

Incubation   Transformation

Present Situation   **Preferred Future**

In this book, you will learn the four stages of the Nehemiah Response Coaching Model™.

The metaphor is a circle moving forward along a line from present situation to the preferred future. The Nehemiah Response Coaching Model™ is a biblical process for transformation. The model captures responses of Nehemiah and will help you develop a custom solution to get from where you are (Present Situation) to where you want to go (Preferred Future).

The Nehemiah Response Coaching Model™ provides a reproducible and repeatable strategic framework for positive change in life and ministry. Application of discoveries made through the four stages of this coaching model will give you traction to move forward.

In the first four chapters of this book, we will focus on the Incubation Stage with a coaching emphasis on the importance of being centered, having a vision, developing a plan, and abiding in faith.

Throughout the coaching process, we will also be referring to the Eight Building Blocks of Coaching from Coaching4Clergy. These building blocks are competencies to include in each coaching session: (1) the coaching agreement, (2) deep listening, (3) powerful questions, (4) action and accountability, (5) the coaching relationship, (6) artful language, (7) creating a new awareness, (8) direct communication.

Powerful Coaching Questions

Preferred Future (see diagram)
- Big picture, what would be your goal?
- What would you like to focus on today?
- When we are done today, what would you like to be able to take away?

Present Situation (see diagram)
- How would you describe your current reality?
- What is happening?
- What's really important?
- What is working, what's not working?

Incubation Stage (see diagram)

- What are some ideas you can put in place?
- What changes will you need to make to get where you want to go?
- Would you like to brainstorm some ideas about how to get there?
- What personal strengths and areas of growth are being revealed during this time?
- What is in the way and keeping you from moving forward?

1 being centered

Those who survived the exile and are back in
the province are in great trouble and disgrace.
The wall of Jerusalem is broken down, and
its gates have been burned with fire. When I
heard these things, I sat down and wept. For
some days, I mourned and fasted and prayed
before the God of heaven.

—Nehemiah 1:3–4

When was the last time you stood on a beach? What were some of your thoughts as you stood watching waves crash along the shoreline? It's amazing how you can almost see the energy and force behind each wave; and yet, those same waves can literally take us away to a magnificent place. A place where we get lost in our own thoughts. A place of peace.

The picture of the beach is a dichotomy—both calming yet powerful, healing yet destructive, beautiful yet very purifying. Honestly, the way you see things—in this case, the beach—depends on your life experiences.

Some of our favorite things are the beautiful beaches and the vast body of water along the Mississippi Gulf Coast. Well, on August 29, 2005, that same body of water turned our lives upside down, and we found ourselves in the middle of one of America's greatest natural disasters—Hurricane Katrina.

Our story could have ended there; however, God chose to take us on an amazing journey, which has changed our lives forever. Out of the rubble of the storm has evolved a book, a ministry, and this coaching model.

We hope to be an encouragement to you on your life's journey. Hopefully, you will never have to face a storm like Hurricane Katrina; however, on a daily basis, we all have opportunities, challenges, or decisions to make. Your decision may be life changing, or it may be a way to get you moving forward again. Wherever you are, whatever the decision is, we hope you find the Nehemiah Response Coaching Model™ a way to move forward in your life.

Where Are You Now and Where Are You Going?

For Nehemiah, it was obvious he was in a state of despair over the destruction of the wall in Jerusalem, and he knew where to turn. It would be nice if answers to life's situations could always be as obvious. For many, we hear, "I'm not sure what is going on in my life, I just feel stuck." Some people tell us they seem to have lost themselves along the way, and they do not know where to turn. For others, they need clarity about their future.

Pause and Ponder
How do you relate?
Where are you now and where are you going?
Big picture, what would you like to focus on in your life?

Being honest about where you are is essential. When was the last time you actually stopped to assess where you are in your life's journey? Often, in coaching, we use the analogy of a carousel. Carousels go round and round with no particular beginning or ending point. Oh, yeah, it may be fun for awhile; however, eventually, it becomes mundane and boring going around endlessly in circles. What would it take for you to unplug the carousel of your life? What might you expect to happen if everything you were doing would come to a halt and you began to make some shifts in your life? Here's a powerful story from one of our coachees, in her own words, about making shifts and being centered.

> Recently, I was asked the question, "What is one thing you might be able to shift in your life this week to lighten the heaviness you currently are experiencing? And, when you figure it out, send me an e-mail!" When I got off the phone, I sat there feeling perplexed. I had no idea what could shift, short of quitting everything I was involved in, and hitting the road to find an elusive cabin in the woods! As I sat there, I soon realized I had to get rid of all my pat answers or "christianese" statements. The truth is, I literally had to sit this one out by

being still, leaning into God, and listening for his still small voice. This was the beginning of becoming aware of how God would perform these subtle shifts in my life. Honestly, to sit still and wait on God's gentle moving in my life is the opposite of my personality. If I see a problem, "I" want to fix it—solve it in three easy steps and be done with it! But from where I was sitting that day, it was evident my three-easy-step plan wasn't going to work this time.

THE COACHING AGREEMENT

Clarifying what the coachee wants to focus on.

So, it's not too early to ask, "Where are you going?" For some reason, this book about a coaching approach, which partners with you through a discovery process, has peaked your interest. You must be on a journey looking for answers. Perhaps you feel a sense of hopelessness and you see this book as the help you need. Maybe, you are hoping to step out and be brave enough to follow a dream you have had for years. Or perhaps, it is a simple decision you need to make by the end of the week in order to improve your job status or heal a broken relationship. Whatever you are considering—no matter how big or how small—you have to know where you are now and where you are going.

What Do You Really Need?

POWERFUL QUESTIONS

Powerful questions promote the exploration of new possibilities and stimulate creativity.

Right now, someone might be saying, "Wow! That's a loaded question!" We would be saying, "Wow! That's a powerful question." The truth is, most of us don't know what we "really need." We may know what we would want to happen, or a lot of us know what we would like to see happen; but to know what we "really need," now, that's a more challenging question to answer. Take any situation where two people do not see eye to eye on a matter and the bottom line is, they haven't a clue what the other person needs to resolve the situation. Most of us want to win in a conflict. If we are honest, we want things to end up going our way—the way we see things. When was the last time you stopped to ask yourself, "What does he need or she need to resolve this issue?

This is not intended to be a lesson on conflict resolution; however, it does bring out a good point—in any situation where a decision is imminent, you may want to ask, "What do you really need?"

What would happen if you decided to reach out to someone? Maybe you need to seek out your pastor, a friend, or a coach. Perhaps, you have heard of someone who has hired a coach, and you are wondering what coaching is all about.

> International Coach Federation defines coaching as partnering with clients in a thought-provoking and creative process that inspires them to maximize their personal and professional potential, which is particularly important in today's uncertain and complex environment. Coaches honor the client as the expert in his or her life and work and believe every client is creative, resourceful, and whole. Standing on this foundation, the coach's responsibility is to:
>
> - Discover, clarify, and align with what the client wants to achieve
> - Encourage client self-discovery
> - Elicit client-generated solutions and strategies
> - Hold the client responsible and accountable

This process helps clients dramatically improve their outlook on work and life, while improving their leadership skills and unlocking their potential.[1]

Steve Ogne and Tim Roehl go as far as suggesting that coaching is the most important format of training in the missional church of the future.[2]

Gary Collins, in his book *Christian Coaching* says:

Coaching is not counseling. It is not for those who need therapy to overcome disruptive painful influences from the past; coaches help people build vision and move toward the future. Coaching is not reactive looking back; it's proactive, looking ahead. It is not about healing; it's about growing. It focuses less on overcoming weaknesses and more on building skills and strengths. Usually, coaching is less formal than the therapist-patient relationship and more of a partnership between two equals, one of whom has experiences, perspectives, or knowledge that can be useful to the other.[3]

Gary Reinecke and Robert Logan say, "Coaching is the process of coming alongside a person or team to help them discover God's agenda for their life and ministry, and then cooperating with the Holy Spirit to see that agenda become a reality."[4]

To summarize coaching, one might say it is an invitation for someone to come alongside a person in their journey. The coach is not there to "fix" anything; he or she is there to guide someone through a discovery process, which brings about change and a preferred future. If you have more questions about coaching, check out the information we have provided for you at our website, www.relevantministry.org/coaching.

Seeking Help Beyond Yourself

Even a fearless leader like Nehemiah sought help beyond himself. The verse we read at the beginning of this chapter gives us insight as to who Nehemiah sought out to help him. It was God. Through the remainder of this book, we will be referring to principles from the book of Nehemiah. You will discover those same principles applied along with the Nehemiah Response Coaching Model™ are transferable; however, for those principles to be beneficial, it is essential you know the God of the principles.

In Nehemiah chapter 1, the layman, Nehemiah, discovered the full extent of what he was about to face. Gripped with the news, he responded, "When I heard these things, I sat down and wept" (Nehemiah 1:4). Then he prayed, "O Lord, God of heaven, the great and awesome God, who keeps his covenant of love ..." (Nehemiah 1:5). Perhaps you are in a similar place as Nehemiah. The decision you have to make has made you weak at the knees, and you want to sit down and cry. How can you include God in your life and experience his promise of love for you?

For us, it was essential to know God was with us as our protector and provider. To this day, whenever we share our Katrina experience, we have to be honest about how scared we were the day of the storm. We were scared about the decision we had made to stay in our home, scared the hurricane force winds or a possible tornado would bring the structure of our house down, and most of all, scared we may never see our family again. It was our personal relationship with God that gave us hope we would make it through the storm. He kept us safe. Going through a storm—experiencing his presence—that's the most important thing.

Choosing to Be Centered

From personal experiences, it seems there are two possible choices people tend to take when faced with a significant decision. They will either run to God or they will run from him. Some may actually go as far as blaming God for what has happened. It's a choice we make to remain centered. Nehemiah chose to run to God by beginning his prayer with praise. He even called God awesome. What do you believe would be your immediate response?

CREATING NEW AWARENESS

Discovering new ways of being and doing.

Next, Nehemiah modeled the character trait of responsibility in his prayer—he repented. Too often, we cringe at the word repentance. The fact is, repentance is not a word we hear or use on a daily basis. For some, it may even conjure up feelings of guilt or conviction. The truth is, repentance is a good word and basically means we are being honest about what we've done wrong and have purposely decided to agree with God by making a dramatic change. Nehemiah said, "I confess" (Nehemiah 1:6). And then he added, "We have acted very wickedly toward you [God]. We have not obeyed the commands" (Nehemiah 1:7).

With repentance, our relationship with God is restored. Repentance toward God is a 180-degree turn to God, and it's good news. The good news about a turn like this for an organizational decision is illustrated in a story Nelson told during a coaching session he had with a leader.

Progress was being made toward this leader's goals, when, during one session, doubt about a next step was expressed because it meant doing something in an entirely different way. Nelson asked, "What if you could turn the 'can't do' into 'can do'? How might those new methods be implemented?" After a long pause, Nelson could see the leader was deep in thought, so he asked the leader if he could share some good news—a repentance story.

To help you picture the setting, Gulfport is sixty miles in both directions with New Orleans to the west and Mobile to the east. "One day, while filling up with gasoline in Gulfport, I struck up a conversation with a man on the other side of the pump. I could tell he was traveling, and he expressed excitement about spending a few days in New Orleans. He said he'd been driving east on Interstate 10 and was looking forward to arriving in New Orleans soon. I realized right away this man needed to be going in the opposite direction. Somewhere along the way, he became disoriented and took a wrong exit."

What was the good news for the traveler? What would he need to do to make a 180-degree turn? If you keep doing things the same way in your organization, what will be the outcome? With the powerful question asked earlier about changing your 'can't do' into a 'can do', there was a breakthrough moment for this leader; which ultimately changed his organization. Just like the example of the man at the gas station, for the leader, changing his thinking to the positive opposite, making a 180-degree turn was definitely good news.

The Eye of the Storm

ARTFUL LANGUAGE

In coaching conversations, we intentionally choose words that are non-manipulative and free of any agenda.

If you are interested in weather, you know the center of a massive storm is called the eye of the storm. The eye of a hurricane is approximately twenty to forty miles in width. These few miles in the midst of a ferocious storm are the only place where you will find calm and beauty. Outside of the center of the storm, you will find massive destruction and incredibly powerful winds; and, pieces of people's lives will be scattered for miles in the torrent of wind and rain. Much like a hurricane, some of the events in our lives make us long for the center of the storm where it is calm and peaceful. The challenge is to be centered.

> ### *Pause and Ponder*
> Where are you right now in your life?
> How close are you to the eye of the storm?

Years ago, we attended a conference on crises management. We'll never forget when the guest speaker asked those going through a crisis to raise their hands. Then he said, "If you're not going through a crisis right now, have you ever experienced a crisis in the past?" And then, this was the most powerful statement he made: "For those of you that have not experienced a crisis, it is not when, it is how you are going to go through your storm."

DIRECT COMMUNICATION

Being clear, concise, and laser-like with words.

You see, most, if not all of us, will go through some kind of a storm in our life. It may not be a literal storm, but it may be an unexpected death in the family that causes added tension, an economic downturn that leads to financial woes, or an unfaithful partner in business or marriage who decides to walk away from his or her commitment. Whatever the storm, it leaves behind a wake of destruction.

We want to encourage you to break through the pressure of the storm like the hurricane hunters do and get centered in the eye of the storm where it is peaceful and beautiful. Whether you are starting a new venture or working through a storm, while you are in the Incubation Stage, centered is where you want to be!

Nehemiah knew God, and he prayed a powerful prayer in Nehemiah chapter 1 following his realization of the condition of Jerusalem. He said, "The great and awesome God, who keeps his covenant of love..." (Nehemiah 1:5). Know this one thing: God loves you just as much as he loved Nehemiah! How will you include him in your life and experience his promise of love for you?

Powerful Questions

What decision do you need to make about your future?

How would you describe your current reality?

What has been your response to God up to this point?

Who do you really need to help you get to where you want to go?

What does the center or the "eye of your storm" look like to you?

What is the next step you would like to take?

POWERFUL QUESTIONS

Powerful questions promote the exploration of new possibilities and stimulate creativity.

2 having a vision

> Lord, the God of heaven, the great and
> awesome God, who keeps his covenant of
> love with those who love him and keep his
> commandments. Let your ear be attentive
> and your eyes open to hear the prayer your
> servant is praying before you day and night.
> —Nehemiah 1:5–6

In chapter 1, we discovered the importance of being honest about where you are right now. We also began the discovery process of where you want to go—your Preferred Future. Along the way in chapter 1, we discussed the importance of being centered during the Incubation Stage and seeking help beyond ourselves. Plus we brainstormed a bit about "what you really need."

ARTFUL LANGUAGE

In coaching conversations, we intentionally choose words that are non-manipulative and free of any agenda.

At this point in the Incubation Stage, you may be experiencing a similar feeling like we did immediately after Hurricane Katrina. We felt like we were on a Lewis and Clark adventure of sorts, with no map to guide us. We found ourselves on a path we'd never walked before—a place where solutions were being discovered as we moved forward. Our hope for you is Nehemiah Response Coaching Model™ can be your map as you make discoveries and move forward.

Vision, Discovering God's Perspective

George Barna's definition for vision in his book, *The Power of Vision*, reads, "Vision for ministry is a clear mental image of a preferable future imparted by God to His chosen servants and is based upon an accurate understanding of God, self and circumstances."[1]

In his book, *Church Unique*, Will Mancini says, "Vision is the living language that anticipates and illustrates God's better intermediate future."[2]

Pause and Ponder
What is it God wants to accomplish through you?
How are you preparing yourself to meet that challenge?

In the Incubation Stage, following the choice to get centered, the next action step is developing a vision. So, how can I discover God's perspective?

When Nehemiah heard of the work that needed to be done in Jerusalem, he pondered and prayed. Nehemiah took time to discover what God had to say about the situation. Nehemiah attempted to see things from God's perspective. Getting started "right" is essential.

Have you ever seen a toddler learning how to dress himself or herself? Their efforts are at best, commendable; however, they don't always get it right the first time. In their early years, we saw some of our grandsons coming out of their rooms so proud they had accomplished getting dressed only to discover they didn't align the buttons on their shirt right, so the shirt appeared to be crooked.

ARTFUL LANGUAGE

In coaching conversations, we intentionally choose words that are non-manipulative and free of any agenda.

The same idea applies when it comes to our perspective versus God's perspective. If we use the analogy of the crooked shirt, our perspective is like the first button missing the first button hole. If we continue to follow suit by buttoning each consecutive button with the same perspective, we may think we are right; but unfortunately, we may be very wrong. However, out of this illustration, we can see the importance between the tension of what is and the reality of the way it could be. How is clarity for your vision born out of the tension of starting right?

ACTION AND ACCOUNTABILITY

Brainstorming, designing the action, and follow through.

We can also learn through Nehemiah's experience, a quick action can often be just a reaction to what is happening in the moment. Nehemiah's first response was to seek out God and see the situation from his perspective. Nehemiah did this before the king released him to go to Jerusalem (Nehemiah 2:7), and when he got to his destination, Nehemiah took time again to survey the site (Nehemiah 2:11–12). Nehemiah was not looking for a "quick fix." Nehemiah desired to be patient and to wait, being careful to align with God's vision. Nehemiah wanted to see things from God's perspective because he believed God's perspective and timing to be imperative.

Who is in your life that is helping you to not just "react" but to respond in the right way? This is where coaching can be so valuable when we have decisions to make. Your coach can partner with you as you move from your current situation to where you want to go. The process of making discoveries along the way can be life changing.

Having a Vision

Recently, Nelson was coaching a church leader who wanted to move forward, but he continued to be stuck in unfulfilled solutions. So, during the session, Nelson used the analogy of a vehicle by asking, "What would be the outcome if you tried to drive your car while only looking at the rearview mirror?" Now consider, what might happen if you spent most of the time looking through the windshield? Just like we look out the windshield of our car to drive, vision is a forward look to the future!

Pause and Ponder

What would you hope to accomplish with this kind of shift? What might be a helpful action for you to discover God's perspective, today?

The Importance of Having a Clear Vision

For several years, we have had "floaters" in our eyes. Floaters are small deposits that form in the back of the eye and cast shadows on the retina. Floaters hinder vision as they appear as small black flicks, spider web like lines, and dark shapes. Most of the time, floaters go unnoticed; but when they drift through the field of sight, they affect a person's vision.

Experiencing floaters causes a person to appreciate having clear vision so much more. Likewise, having a great optometrist who keeps watch on the situation is similar to the relationship we have with God and our spiritual vision. This is where a coach could help you with a new awareness about a clear perspective along your journey.

Our physical sight, or vision, is probably the most important sense we have. But no matter how wonderful it is, our physical sight can only see physical reality. Spiritual vision is perceiving spiritual reality—God's perspective or what he has in mind. Spiritual vision involves the plans God has for you. It's about where you are going and what it's going to look like when you get there. This is vision.

Pause and Ponder

What, like floaters, keeps you from seeing God's plan clearly?
What do you believe God is calling you to do?
What are your challenges in connecting with God?
How are you able to clearly see the plans God has in mind for you?

What Needs to Happen Today?

Spiritual vision can be hindered by the busyness in our lives. How often are you, like the coachee in chapter 1, in a hurry to try to "fix" the problem or put a quick plan together before earnestly seeking God? Nehemiah made the decision to take some time and so, he prayed some days. For him, action was not the first response. Instead, Nehemiah was patient during his Incubation Stage of sorts, and God revealed his vision to Nehemiah at just the right time.

Imagine a gallon jar of water filled with mud and other sediments in front of you. What happens when you swirl it around? How well can you see through the jar? What would happen if you would set the jar down for a day or two? Allowing the floaters to settle to the bottom takes time.

How is your vision becoming clearer for you? That's a good question to ask when you want to move forward with a clear vision during a transition.

CREATING NEW AWARENESS

Discovering new ways of being and doing.

An added benefit of taking time is assessing personal needs. In chapter 1, we found Nehemiah in the middle of a prayer to God. In verse 7, he gets honest about human failure. Here, we learn the purpose of taking time can also be for self-evaluation by asking the following question. What personal strengths and areas of growth are being revealed in my life during this time? Your answers may be critical to moving forward into the vision God is revealing.

One more thing to note, we find Nehemiah being joined by others in his time of need. In chapter 1, when Nehemiah prayed in response to the condition of Jerusalem, he evidently had some prayer partners. "O Lord, let your ear be attentive to the prayer of this your servant and to the prayer of your servants who delight in revering your name" (Nehemiah 1:11). When Nehemiah arrived in Jerusalem, before he announced his plan to rebuild publicly, he surveyed the city with others. He said in the second chapter, "I set out during the night with a few men" (Nehemiah 2:12).

Pause and Ponder
How good of a team player are you?
As you get traction and move forward, how open are you to receiving help from someone else?
Who do you have in your life you can confide in or brainstorm with?

What is God's plan, his vision for you? According to Andy Stanley, "Vision is a clear mental picture of what could be, fueled by the conviction that it should be. Vision is a preferred future. A destination."[3] You may have an answer, but if not, remain in the Incubation Stage. Obviously, Nehemiah was fueled by his conviction to seek God spending at least one hundred days in his Incubation Stage. What might have been his feelings on day sixty or day seventy-five? We know he kept on. How about you?

Beware of Withdrawal and Isolation

Have you ever noticed, as the vision is becoming clearer, whether you are starting a new venture or coming out of a challenging time, there is the possibility of being driven inward? The emotions of uncertainty, confusion, sadness, and hurt make it hard to open up and reach out; let alone get started with what really needs to be done. We are convinced this is a point where you need at least one true friend. Someone you can trust. Someone you will allow to get close to you during times of decision-making.

Likewise, isolation, whether we do it to ourselves or if it's done to us, is something to get beyond. Often, we need someone else to speak words of encouragement to us.

THE COACHING RELATIONSHIP

Presence - a deeper level of knowing.

With both withdrawal and isolation, we see a lack of trust. Trust is earned; and those who are skeptical, or have experienced hurt may have trust issues. Remember, as a coach, to take time in the Incubation Stage to be patient and wait for trust to be built in the relationship between you and the person you are coaching.

Graciously, one of Pam's coachees has given us permission to share her story about the isolation caused in her life through walls that she had built. Through an arduous process of building trust and becoming vulnerable the walls came crumbling down.

> I have always sensed that I wasn't an easy person to get to know. What I didn't realize was how I had developed such an effective defense mechanism growing up in an ever changing environment. Plus, I didn't fully comprehend how my defensive nature was affecting my life, my family, and most of all, my relationship with my Heavenly Father.
>
> Gratefully, God intervened and I set out on a coaching adventure. Through that intercession, I started down a path of discovery that allowed me to take an honest look at myself. The coaching process encouraged me to evaluate "who I am" and "where I'd like to be." During our coaching sessions, I was able to set goals, create healthy boundaries, and have a safe environment to grow.

As our coaching relationship grew deeper and a greater trust was developed, the depth of my "guarded self" was exposed. Since that point, I have made tremendous progress from when I first began this journey.

Recently, I shared with an intimate group of Christian women what it felt like for me to be guarded. The best way to describe it was that I had built huge walls all around me to keep people out. The image I had was that one by one, people were trying to make it over the wall and infiltrate my life and my heart. That certainly isn't a picture of God's best for me! So once again, I was able to see how unhealthy it was to be so defensive. That night, I discovered when I block people out that I fear will hurt me, I am also blocking out those who could love me or people who possibly need my help.

There's no way to fully express the breakthrough that was made without personally experiencing it. I can truly say that the coaching approach has proven invaluable in my life; and I'm certain the people in my life could attest to that!

Hopefully, this testimony has shed some light on the importance of building trust with the person you are coaching. Remember, trust takes time and time builds the coaching relationship, which nourishes a healthy environment for someone to grow in. Together, your coachee will discover new opportunities and gain a new awareness about the way things could be in the future.

What One Step Could You Take Today?

Do you have some important decisions to make? Look to God; see it from his perspective. Discover what God may be doing in your situation. Do your best to get in step with him. Also, look around and be open to receive what someone close by may have to offer to help you where you're at right now. Our prayer is that you might be blessed in your own Nehemiah response.

So, putting details aside, what is God's plan or his idea for you? Once you have nailed that down, you can begin to think about the details. So how does a plan come together? How do you make decisions while developing a plan? Let's take that step in chapter 3.

Powerful Questions

What steps have you taken to seek God's perspective in your decision-making process?

What is keeping you from seeing things clearly?

What is your natural response to "act" or "react"?

What is your tendency to isolate yourself during important decision-making times?

What is the next step you would like to take?

Who are the people you can trust with your "guarded self"?

How would it benefit you to work with a coach?

POWERFUL QUESTIONS

Powerful questions promote the exploration of new possibilities and stimulate creativity.

3 developing a plan

Come, let us rebuild the wall of Jerusalem,
and we will no longer be in disgrace. I also
told them about the gracious hand of my God
upon me and what the king had said to me.
—Nehemiah 2:17–18

In the mid-1980s, a popular television program was called The A-Team. In each episode, the team found themselves in challenging situations. Prior to the team's critical mission, they would always say—what became the show's famous line, "I love it when a plan comes together."

ARTFUL LANGUAGE

In coaching conversations, we intentionally choose words that are non-manipulative and free of any agenda.

Just like in the episodes of the A-Team, the next step in moving forward is the development of a plan. Once we've resolved God has a plan, it's our job to begin making plans that align with his plan.

The day of opportunity came for Nehemiah to share his heart with the king. Nehemiah, a captive of Babylon, was employed as the cupbearer for King Artaxerxes (Nehemiah 2:1) in the citadel of Susa (Nehemiah 1:1) about eight hundred miles to the east of Jerusalem. Nehemiah had been praying for over one hundred days (Nehemiah 1:1 "month of Kislev," Nehemiah 2:1 "month of Nisan"), and God orchestrated a right-time/right-place moment. The king said, "What is it you want?" (Nehemiah 2:4)

Nehemiah responded, "If it pleases the king and if your servant has found favor in his sight, let him send me to the city in Judah where my fathers are buried so that I can rebuild it" (Nehemiah 2:5).

The door of opportunity was now open, and as the conversation continued, Nehemiah was able to share the plan that had come together during his Incubation Stage. Nehemiah knew what to ask for because he had been spending time with God. He also had been praying with a few other people along the same lines.

Nehemiah asked to be sent, and it was granted to him. Because Nehemiah had been praying and planning, he knew what he needed to get started. Once the king asked the powerful question, "What do you want?" Nehemiah answered by requesting specific provisions and protection, and the king gave it to him.

Nehemiah knew he was in step with God's plan, "Because the gracious hand of my God was upon me, the king granted my requests" (Nehemiah 2:8).

How Do You Put a Plan Together?

The vision we have will be just a dream until we develop a plan. The plan makes the vision tangible. Here are some important considerations about planning from verses in Nehemiah chapter 2:

- (v.1) Continue to be faithful in your current work while making future plans. Nehemiah was loyal to his current responsibilities while he was praying and planning for the future.

- (v.2) Wait patiently for the right time to share what is on your heart. God opened the door for Nehemiah when the king initiated by asking the question, "Why does your face look so sad?"

- (v.3) When asked, share your heart with confidence. Nehemiah's planning during his Incubation Stage gave him confidence.

- (v.4) When the door of opportunity opens, rely on God. Nehemiah's quick prayer was not to ask God what to say "in the moment," but to have the courage to say what was already placed in his heart by God. Nehemiah definitely had something to say because he had been seeking God and thinking things through.

- (v.5) Wins happen when opportunity and preparation meet. For more than a hundred days, Nehemiah had been praying and planning. The two are good go-togethers—praying and planning—they help facilitate the intersection of opportunity and preparation.

Nehemiah's approach to planning involved the following four parts—rest, reflection, rallying support, and remaining flexible. What can we learn from him in each of these areas?

Rest Isn't Optional

When Nehemiah arrived in Jerusalem, he rested three days. I know what you're thinking: You've got to be kidding, right? Are you saying that Nehemiah arrived on the scene and he didn't do anything? Granted, there was so much to do; however, they had just completed an eight-hundred-mile journey, which probably took around four months. The trip was exhausting. They rested, which was the most important thing needed at the time. With this, we can learn the importance of balance in our lives and the power of self-care. The following story is from a ministry leader on a journey of learning the importance of self-care.

> I had been talking about the possibility of connecting for life coaching sessions for months. I finally said, "Sure, why not..." However, even after I said yes, it took me another month just to follow through with

setting up the first appointment. Life is so busy! Putting off such a great opportunity due to busyness had become my MO (method of operation). I'm not even sure I realized how much I needed coaching, at that time, but God has a way of getting our attention.

For me, being in ministry was making it difficult to find time free from distractions to be alone with the Lord. However, early one morning, while studying and praying, I sensed the Lord telling me to slow down and focus on what I was called to do in the Body of Christ. I cried out to the Lord, "How? When there are so many other things I need to take care of...important things—things no one else can or will do." But God wouldn't let these thoughts go, and immediately, I began to think of areas in my life that overwhelm me. Things that seemed to be keeping me from focusing on the ministry God had been calling me to do.

It was then; I realized how valuable life coaching can be. Within a week, after the first coaching session, I had identified at least one area of my life where I could make some changes to relieve stress and give me more time to focus on what God was calling me to do. I began working on a plan to train others; and release and empower them into ministry areas where I once served. Now, I have more time for self-care and ministry. I have a long way to go, but progress is being made as I stay focused and rest in the Lord.

Coaches, the Incubation Stage is a great place for us to model the importance of self-care. When you show up for a session, how rested and ready are you in order to be fully present for the person you are meeting? We live in a world where everyone is moving at a breakneck pace. We're so busy oriented. As we consider the idea that rest isn't optional, ponder the concept Richard Foster shares in his book, *Freedom of Simplicity*, about self-care.

THE COACHING RELATIONSHIP

Presence - a deeper level of knowing.

I function best when I alternate between periods of intense activity and of comparative solitude. When I understand this about myself, I can order my life accordingly. After a certain amount of immersion in public life, I begin to burn out. And I have noticed that I burn out inwardly long before I do outwardly. Hence, I must be careful not to become a frantic bundle of hollow energy, busy among people but devoid of life...I must learn to retreat, like Jesus, and experience the recreating power of God...Along our journey we need to discover numerous tarrying places where we can receive heavenly manna.[1]

In a decision-making process, all that needs to be done is multiplied, and it helps for us to know our limits. With the understanding we all need rest, we will be able to accomplish what our physical bodies are capable of doing. Busyness can also cause us to disconnect from God. Realizing the importance of a balanced life, we are convinced that rest is not optional.

Taking time for our physical needs is like sharpening our edge. Likewise, we see that Nehemiah rested. Then, before he publicly laid out the plan, he reflected and reviewed the status of the work to be done. So after three days of rest, Nehemiah said, "I set out during the night with a few men. I had not told anyone what my God had put in my heart to do for Jerusalem" (Nehemiah 2:12).

Honest Reflection

In chapter 2, our focus was on having a vision. In this chapter, our theme is planning, which involves taking time for honest reflection. Vision is about where you are going. Plans are how you are going to get where you are going!

The process of planning helps us to think things through, which produces possible outcomes. Buildings exist because an architect assessed the needs, gathered the facts, and did research. This is the process of advanced planning. In much the same way, planning is an important part of life and ministry.

> ## THE COACHING AGREEMENT
>
> Clarifying what the coachee wants to focus on.

Planning is an important part and one of the responses in what we are calling an Incubation Stage in the Nehemiah Response Coaching Model™. Before we take action, it is best to plan and set goals; otherwise, we may respond with a knee-jerk reaction instead of a well-thought-through process. Planning comes after getting God's vision and before moving forward. If Nehemiah was your coach, he might encourage you to do some brainstorming around opportunities and possible obstacles, and then he may help you discover and design your action steps while in the Incubation Stage. Through the coaching process, you may become anxious to move forward. Let us encourage you to see the benefit in waiting until you feel confident the plan has come together.

> ## ACTION AND ACCOUNTABILITY
>
> Brainstorming, designing the action, and follow through.

Rallying Support

Once Nehemiah rested and after he reflected on the situation, he then rallied the support he needed. Rallying is to renew an effort or to arouse action. It's about pulling together, joining a common cause and crossing the finish line.

Think about it for a minute. Morale was probably at an all-time low for the people in Jerusalem. Their city wall was broken. Their homes were in need of repair. Discouragement and skepticism could have overruled. They could have said something like:

"Who is this guy?"

"Where did he come from?"

"Who does he think he is?"

"Rebuild this wall? We've already tried that."

"He's asking us to do the impossible!"

But they didn't. They responded to Nehemiah's rallying call to rebuild by saying, "Let us start rebuilding. So they began this good work" (Nehemiah 2:18).

What did Nehemiah say to get such a response? Here it is:

> Then I said to them, "You see the trouble we are in: Jerusalem lies in ruins, and its gates have been burned with fire. Come, let us rebuild the wall of Jerusalem, and we will no longer be in disgrace." I also told them about the gracious hand of my God upon me and what the king had said to me. (Nehemiah 2:17–18)

Nehemiah asked the people to see what he saw. The problem was plainly and honestly defined. The solution was simply stated, and then he asked them to own the work, "Come, let us rebuild" (Nehemiah 2:17). He reminded them it was their wall, too. He made it clear he didn't come to Jerusalem to rebuild the wall by himself. Nehemiah wanted them to know, if we're going to do this, we've got to do it together. It is God's mission and idea, not mine. I'm his servant. And because it's God's idea, he will give us the victory. It's an awesome thing when a plan comes together!

Pause and Ponder
How does all of this fit with your situation?
How do you find time for rest?
What action steps do you need to take based on what you know?
How can you and your team rally and move forward?

Remain Flexible

Do you remember the flexible toy called Gumby? Well, we have a similar toy around our house, only it is a long, wiry rabbit. Recently, we pulled him out to remind us we need to remain flexible—flexible not only to change, but also to interruptions.

Does this ever happen to you? You have a plan. You know exactly what you want to accomplish, but then it doesn't work out the way you hoped it would. You know the saying: "The best laid plans of men and mice often go askew." That's exactly how we felt. From the moment our feet hit the ground, it seemed to be one interruption or distraction after another. None of which were bad things, just a detour in the day that was already planned.

Pause and Ponder

What do you do when things don't go the way you planned?
How do you feel when things seem out of control?
What is your response to the people who seem to be keeping you from the task at hand?
How do you keep from going to extremes and find middle ground to stay flexible?
What is the secret to being open to change in your life and not frustrated with interruptions?

Let's use the wiry rabbit as an illustration. If we take the rabbit and twist his arms and legs and get him to look frustrated, he will appear to be closed to new ideas or relationships. He may also look uncomfortable with himself and those around him. Think about it, when we let some insignificant thing get us all uptight, we shut down any possibility of accepting a new or different way to approach things. It might be much harder to change our course if we get hung up on what "should be" instead of the way it "could be."

ARTFUL LANGUAGE

In coaching conversations, we intentionally choose words that are non-manipulative and free of any agenda.

Now, let's go to the opposite side of this scenario. What would happen if the rabbit's lanky arms and legs were pulled straight out and he was placed in a lying down position? Wouldn't that suggest that he has just given up? What do you do when you feel overwhelmed? Do you say, "I can't get this done, it's too big of a project, or there are too many obstacles. I'm just going to quit!" Maybe you become quiet and withdrawn from those who are dear to you. The message is, "Change isn't going to happen any time soon."

We are all aware that life is filled with both changes and interruptions. The question is, "How good are you at accepting it?"

Pause and Ponder
What steps do you need to take to be able to overcome an interruption or face change?
What can you do when you feel knocked off of dead center?
What adjustments do you make to keep your
plan moving forward?

May we offer some suggestions that have worked for others as far as remaining flexible?

- Start with the plan, knowing interruptions or the need for change may happen.

- Find the opportunity in a challenging situation.

- Be open to thinking outside the box.

- Exercise self-control by finding your center. (What gives you a sense of peace?)

- Accept responsibility for your actions, and don't blame others for the interruptions in your life.

- Realize, complaining will keep you fixated on the problem, not help you find a solution.

- Remember, you have a choice in the matter.

Four planning action steps emerged from this chapter. Nehemiah rested, he reflected, rallied support for appropriate action, and he remained flexible.

Before we move any further, there is an interesting dynamic to address. There's something else out there that is likely to come along during a time of decision-making. Maybe you've experienced it already. It's fear. Where does fear come from? What will it do to you? Let's explore more in chapter 4.

Powerful Questions

How can you turn your tendency to react into a right action for planning?

Why do you think rest is so important?

What reflection or research would help you in your situation?

"To rally" shows action. What action do you need to take, today?

How will you remain flexible when needed?

POWERFUL QUESTIONS

Powerful questions promote the exploration of new possibilities and stimulate creativity.

4 abiding in faith

The king asked me, "Why does your face look
so sad when you are not ill? This can be nothing
but sadness of heart." I was very much afraid.
—Nehemiah 2:2–3

You're ready to move forward, to take action and
implement your plan, but something rises up to the
contrary. You know God is leading, but opposition to
the plan happens. Perhaps the opposition is coming
from you, or it might be coming from others. Maybe
you are being challenged by your own self-doubt, with
questions like, "What are you thinking? What you are
about to do is too big or it's so different it can't be
done." Or, it could be coming from others who are
saying, "How do you think you are going to accomplish
this venture when you never seem to finish anything you
start?" Immediately, fear sets in, faith vanishes, and you

begin to believe the opposing voice within or the voices of others.

Facing Opposition

Fear could have gripped Nehemiah and stopped him from speaking altogether, or at least saying what God had put on his heart. Fear could have kept the work from ever starting. As soon as they agreed to rebuild the wall, opposers who heard about it "mocked and ridiculed" Nehemiah (Nehemiah 2:19).

CREATING NEW AWARENESS

Discovering new ways of being and doing.

Instead of being gripped with fear, Nehemiah's faith was strong when he encountered the opposition. Despite being mocked and ridiculed, he remained steadfast as he began the building project. Just like Nehemiah, you too can count on opposition at the start of something new. God's leading and blessing does not necessarily mean there will be no opposition to plans for moving forward into the future.

However, notice how Nehemiah responded in verse 20. Nehemiah stayed focused and did not engage in conversation with his opposers over their mocking and ridicule, instead:

- He honored God, saying, "We will be successful, and God will be the reason for success."

- Then he stated his role as a servant and declared his intentions to get started.

- And he was not alone in his actions of faith. He said, "God will give us success...we his servants will start rebuilding."

Nehemiah kept his focus in the right place and on the right things when opposition could have brought fear and halted action. "What's This about Fear?" is the title of chapter 4 in the book, *Nehemiah Response: How to Make It Through Your Crisis*. The following excerpt is from pages 58–59. This short story is about a time when we were in a similar situation and how opposition stirred our inner fears about plans for the future.

> Six days after Katrina, Pam and I found ourselves in line with thousands of other people to receive the basic essentials of life: water, ice, and MREs (meals ready to eat). It was at that moment that all that had happened in the preceding days became reality. This really happened; it's not a dream. I'm standing in a distribution line with my wife.
>
> That day in particular, while in the distribution line, it hit me with a punch that seemed as hard as Katrina herself and the waves of fear rippled through my mind. It wasn't the National Guard

standing armed and at their posts—their presence was actually reassuring. It was an eerie feeling, almost like being in the middle of a dream, but it wasn't a dream. Previously, I had felt a numbness which kept me from accepting the situation, but on this day, it became a reality.

Fear is something that will keep you from taking action. Fear is something that can prevent any further progress. We came to realize that there's a big task ahead of us, and we can be overwhelmed by it all. The thing that could have kept Nehemiah from moving out from where he was, was expressed as fear. He had never been where he was before, and he was afraid. He was standing at the threshold of a lot of things to tackle, and maybe his emotions were numb to some things, but he felt fear.

What are you afraid of today? What are some of the fears we can have when we're ready to launch out on a new venture? How about self-doubt, uncertainty, a lack of confidence, just to name a few fears. You'll have to discover what causes fear in you. But know this for sure: you'll have to overcome your fears to move forward.[1]

Abiding in Faith

Pause and Ponder

What are some of the ways, you are able to overcome fear?
If you are ready to move forward, how can you be ready
to face opposition?

Who or What is Holding You Captive?

In the 70s, Nelson served as a youth pastor, and some of the high school students from our youth group performed, *For This Cause*, a powerful play about missionaries, John and Betty Stamm, who served in China in 1934. During that period of Chinese history, it was not uncommon for bandits to come into towns to kidnap people for a ransom or to vandalize and then murder their victims. To these bandits, foreigners were seen as wealthy so this young, American missionary couple became one of their preys.

As we think about fear and faith, we are reminded about a poem from the play spoken by Betty before she was murdered. Although the poem, by E. H. Hamilton, was not written about the Stamm's merciless murder, it was actually written about another martyred missionary, Jack W. Vinsen. As you read the words to this poem, consider what the "bandit" is that may be holding you captive.

ARTFUL LANGUAGE

In coaching conversations, we intentionally choose words that are non-manipulative and free of any agenda.

Afraid? Of what?
To feel the spirit's glad release?
To pass from pain to perfect peace,
The strife and strain of life to cease?
Afraid? Of that?

Afraid? Of what?
Afraid to see the Savior's face,
To hear His welcome, and to trace,
The glory gleam from wounds of grace,
Afraid? Of that?

Afraid? Of what?
A flash–a crash–a pierced heart;
Brief darkness–Light–O Heaven's art!
A wound of His a counterpart!
Afraid? Of that?

Afraid? Of what?
To enter into Heaven's rest,
And yet to serve the Master blessed?
From service good to service best?
Afraid? Of that?

Afraid? Of what?
To do by death what life could not
Baptize with blood a stony plot,
Till souls shall blossom from the spot?
Afraid? Of that?[2]

Pause and Ponder

What requires faith in your life right now?
How is fear keeping you from stepping out?
Who could help you in your discovery process?

Getting Beyond Your Fears

As we begin to wrap up our final thoughts about the Incubation Stage in the Nehemiah Response Coaching Model™, it is important to remember fear may cause you to get stuck, and you may want to hold on to some limiting beliefs or false assumptions.

> ## CREATING NEW AWARENESS
> Discovering new ways of being and doing.

Throughout the coaching process, we have discovered that both limiting beliefs and false assumptions can stagnate the possibility of moving forward from the Incubation Stage to the Implementation Stage. In his book, Accelerated Coach Training, J. Val Hastings, states, "Everyone has beliefs and assumptions; and they show up in coaching all of the time." Hastings goes on to explain just how powerful beliefs and assumptions can be. He gives a list including:

- Beliefs and assumptions can propel us forward or paralyze us.

- Beliefs and assumptions can expand our options or limit our choices.

- Beliefs and assumptions can rally one to take initiative or to throw in the towel.[3]

In the story of Nehemiah, we find him moving ahead when fear could have paralyzed him. In chapter 2, verse 2 Nehemiah said, "I was very much afraid;" however, because of his confidence in God and the plan which had been revealed to him, he made a faith response!

According to J. Val Hastings, limiting beliefs and false assumptions have gained power because they have gone unquestioned.[4]

Pause and Ponder

What challenges are you facing in moving forward because limiting beliefs are causing fear to rise up in you?
Who is encouraging you with some powerful questions to get you past those false assumptions?
If you were not limited by fear, what would you be able to do?

A perfect illustration comes to mind from a coaching session. One of the resources we use as an assessment tool is the Wheel of Life—it is commonly used for goal setting. The exercise provides a visual representation of how satisfied you are with various key aspects of your life. The person is to label each section of the wheel from eight areas of their life and then place a value between one to ten, with ten being the greatest, in each section. Once the wheel is completed, it reflects what the person values most and how much energy they are expending in that particular area of their life.[5]

While in a session with a coachee, Pam asked, about an area that was marked particularly low—health and fitness. When asked to share more about the value she had placed on health and fitness, the coachee began to explain how she felt hopeless. She said, "I'm overweight, I have all kinds of health issues going on, and my life is busy, so I don't exercise."

Hoping to encourage the coachee, Pam asked, "What one step do you think you could take right now to improve this area in your life?" Immediately, tears began to flow. There was definitely more to the story. You see, the person had just suffered the loss of several family members within a six-week time period all because of similar health-related issues.

Through the tears, the coachee said, "I could begin by making a doctor's appointment. I need to have some tests done, and I want to work on getting my health back." Wow! That seemed like a major step; until, Pam asked this question, "How motivated are you to take that step?" With that question, you could see it on her face, limiting beliefs and false assumptions set in. With her head down, she said, "I'm not motivated. It doesn't seem to matter if I go to the doctor or not, I'm going to die just like everyone else in my family." The power of fear had definitely gripped her.

Fortunately, as she worked through the process, she realized her husband and family could be a good support system for her, and she decided to call the doctor the next day to set up the appointment for a complete physical exam. Limiting beliefs and false assumptions are powerful, as false assumptions set us up to operate in fear instead of faith. Unfortunately, fear limits our effectiveness; however, having someone to support and encourage us in our life can be just as powerful. And as coaches, we are able to create the space where the person can make their own discoveries, which in turn, empower their thoughts.

Just like we saw in the previous example, our fears can be very real and challenging. Here are three steps to consider overcoming fear:

1. *Realize* fear has power.

2. *Identify* the object of your fear. Is it the fear of failure? The fear of what others might be thinking? Fear has an object. What are you afraid of and why?

3. *Focus* on the truth about the situation.

What have been the effects of fear on your faith? Interestingly, often the things we fear are really insignificant. As we wrap up this chapter and get ready to shift to the Implementation Stage, here are some questions to ponder.

Powerful Questions

What do you want to accomplish?

What might you be assuming?

Who or what is stirring up limiting beliefs?

How motivated are you to accomplish your goal?

POWERFUL QUESTIONS

Powerful questions promote the exploration of new possibilities and stimulate creativity.

PART 2

implementation stage

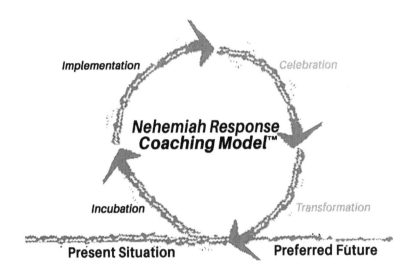

A question that often comes up at this point is, "How much time is dedicated to working through each of the stages of the Nehemiah Response Coaching Model™?"

The Nehemiah Response Coaching Model™ provides flexibility because it isn't meant to be restricted to a linear process. Each situation will be unique. Working through the entire process of the model could range from a few minutes to start your day, if you are doing self coaching, to months when you are coaching a person through an individual goal or an organization through a strategic plan.

When we consider the amount of time allowed for the Incubation Stage compared to the Implementation Stage for Nehemiah, it is quite interesting to see the results.

The amount of time Nehemiah spent in seeking God, praying and planning are recorded in chapter 1 of the book of Nehemiah. In chapter 1, verse 1, there is reference for a month of the year for the calendar used in Nehemiah's day. Then, in chapter 2, verse 1, a month of the year is mentioned just before he speaks with the king. According to these months, Nehemiah spent approximately one hundred days in what we refer to as the Incubation Stage. Looking ahead to Nehemiah 6:15, we learn the wall of Jerusalem was rebuilt in just fifty-two days.

Realizing the difference of a hundred days and fifty-two days, we might consider, "What does this ratio say to you about the importance of time spent in the Incubation Stage?"

In the next four chapters, we will focus on a coaching approach for starting strong, overcoming challenges, serving others, and finishing well during the Implementation Stage.

Powerful Coaching Questions

Implementation Stage (see diagram)
- What will you do over the next two weeks?

- What would you like to be able to tell me when we get together next time?
- How have you prioritized your action steps?
- What will be a first step for you?
- How determined are you to reach your goal?

5 starting strong

They replied, "Let us start rebuilding." So, they
began this good work.

—Nehemiah 2:18

Athletes realize that achievement is as much mental as it is physical. Some athletes may apply the mental strategy of self-talk. You might hear them saying, "I can do this." "I just need to push through."

When you compare yourself to an athlete, what action steps might you want to add to your agenda today? What strategies do you have in place to insure you will start your race? In the Nehemiah Response Coaching Model™; you will discover a biblical, transformational process for gaining traction and moving forward. In the previous chapters, we worked through the Incubation Stage. We looked at the importance of being centered, having a vision, developing a plan, and abiding in faith by overcoming fear.

Within the next four chapters, we will look at the Implementation Stage of the Nehemiah Response Coaching Model™. Specifically, we will look at the importance of taking action in this chapter.

Putting the Plan into Action

Nehemiah and the workers were finally ready to implement the plan; they took action. Like the example of an athlete, we see Nehemiah had a strategy for the work to be done in rebuilding the wall. Nehemiah was ready to put his plan into action.

ACTION AND ACCOUNTABILITY

Brainstorming, designing action, and follow through.

Here are Nehemiah's three strategies for action to consider found in Nehemiah chapter 3:

1. *Teamwork.* The people worked together in specific groups. The phrase, "next to them/him is found twenty-eight times." There are forty-four groups of people mentioned, and they are positioned strategically in a total of forty-two places to do the work and carry out the plan. Who could be a part of your team to help you and hold you accountable?

2. *Prioritizing.* There were ten gates around the wall, which were in need of repair, and each are mentioned in a counterclockwise order beginning and ending at the Sheep Gate. Each was repaired in a systematic order. The Sheep Gate speaks not only of what's first, but who's first. The Sheep Gate provided access for the sheep pasturing in the northern hills outside of Jerusalem to come into the city. From this gate, it was a short distance to the temple where they were offered as sacrifices. Interestingly, it was through this same gate Jesus Christ entered during Passion Week; which ended with the cross and his sacrifice.

3. *Inside-Out.* They began the work where they were. They took action beginning at their own house. There was a lot to do. Instead of being overwhelmed they began where they were and proceeded out from there.

To illustrate the principle of inside-out, we would like to share a parable written by Russell Conwell, a minister; and university founder and president in Philadelphia in the early 1900s. Acres of Diamonds originated as a speech, which Conwell delivered over six thousand times around the world.[1]

THE COACHING AGREEMENT

Clarifying what the coachee wants to focus on.

The central idea of the parable is that one need not look too far from home for opportunity or achievement. In the parable, a man desperately wanted to find diamonds; so, he sold his property, left his family, and journeyed off in search for diamonds. Years later, when he returned to his hometown—old, tired, and poor—he discovered the new owner of his house had found diamonds in the backyard of the property. If only he had applied the principle of inside–out, he could have been a rich man by never leaving his own backyard.

Beware, Perfectionism Can Paralyze

As an elementary student, Nelson stuttered. According to him, there were certain words that seemed to get stuck in his head, making them hard to get out. Stuttering was a real problem for him, often causing him to feel humiliated. As a young boy, having a conversation with anyone was an anxiety-filled experience. He would have to go through the process of thinking and rethinking how to say something, hoping the words would come out right. Often, in an effort to avoid embarrassment, he would just avoid saying anything at all.

After a period of time, he convinced himself it was best not to speak unless he could correctly pronounce all of the words. Because he was so afraid of making a mistake, he set up a standard of perfectionism for himself. Increasingly, as time went on, he had to overcome both the fear of making mistakes and trying to be perfect.

CREATING NEW AWARENESS

Discovering new ways of being and doing.

As time passed and his speech improved, he would quickly recover from the mistakes and would continue the conversation. Eventually, Nelson overcame his stuttering. He said, "I came to see that being concerned about saying words perfectly and what others were thinking about me kept me from speaking at all."

Overcoming stuttering has challenged him to see the importance of taking action and moving forward. Now, Nelson coaches himself by asking thought-provoking questions. "Why should I let my fear of a mistake keep me from taking action?" "Why will I let a desire for everything to be perfect paralyze me?"

Nelson's childhood experience of stuttering is a great illustration of a potentially paralyzing behavior of inaction when it's time to implement an initiative. So, when you are at a crossroad in your decision-making, what action steps will you implement?

Another key factor we see from this illustration is the importance of timing and being confident to move forward. So, when you have clarity about where you are going; and, if there is a good plan in place to get there, it's time for action!

Pause and Ponder

What action steps do you need to put into place?
What might be holding you back?
How might perfectionism keep you from moving forward?

The action plan for Nehemiah, for us, and for you calls for creating teams, prioritizing, and beginning where you are. With this in mind, we must know that everything won't come easy. Things worthwhile are worth working for, and that work has its daily challenges. In the next chapter, we will consider persevering through the Implementation Stage.

Powerful Questions

What would be the benefits of working as a team?

What makes working as a team difficult?

How have you prioritized your action steps?

How does the inside-out principle apply to you and your situation?

POWERFUL QUESTIONS

Powerful questions promote the exploration of new possibilities and stimulate creativity.

6 overcoming challenges

Don't be afraid of them. Remember the Lord,
who is great and awesome, and fight for your brothers,
your sons and your daughters, your wives and
your homes...they did their work with
one hand and held a weapon in the other.
—Nehemiah 4:14, 17

When the wall of Jerusalem had reached half of its height (Nehemiah 4:6), daily challenges began to come in the form of opposition for Nehemiah. Opposition and resistance came from those who did not want to see the wall of Jerusalem rebuilt. For Nehemiah, he was literally up against people who did not want the project to succeed. The opposition and resistance became so obvious that Nehemiah talked about a particular individual who "became angry and was greatly incensed" (Nehemiah 4:1) when he heard of the rebuilding. This person used words to *ridicule* the work.

Remaining Focused

So, what is the significance of opposition and resistance happening at the halfway point? Where are you at on your journey between your start and your finish? For some, you may be at a point where you are tired and just want to give up; and for others, challenges may be spurring you on to be even more determined to finish the goal.

THE COACHING AGREEMENT

Clarifying what the coachee wants to focus on.

Well, that's exactly what happened for Nehemiah. Instead of buckling under to these naysayers, Nehemiah said, "He and 'the people worked with all their heart'" (Nehemiah 4:6). Nehemiah along with the people made a conscientious decision to remain focused and face their challenges. Together, they determined to keep on with the work of rebuilding with their whole heart. According to Linda J. Miller and Chad W. Hall, coaching is a collaborative journey toward the goals of the person(s) being coached.1 Looks like Nehemiah was being a good coach.

Ultimately, their determination not only helped them to overcome the negative atmosphere they were in, it also helped them to remain focused and move forward with even more determination in what the Lord had called them to do—their Preferred Future, finishing the wall.

Overcoming Challenges

We have a coachee who has horses and used this imagery in the following story about the importance of remaining focused and being spurred on to move forward.

> Being in a coaching relationship has been like a spur for me. Powerful questions challenge me to think and get me going in a forward direction. Now, I know that most people think of spurs as harsh instruments to punish a horse; but that's not true. I guess, like any tool, spurs could be used that way, but they are not intended for that purpose. Ask any real cowboy, he will tell you that spurs are an important part of his riding equipment. The key to being a good spur is getting a horse (or in this case, me) to overcome challenges and move forward by holding me accountable for my actions so I can reach my goal.

THE COACHING RELATIONSHIP

Presence - a deeper level of knowing.

In the book of Nehemiah, we see "The people worked with all their heart" (Nehemiah 4:6) and became even more determined because they persevered through their challenges. They were steadfast and resolved to see the job finished.

Know this one thing for sure, if you set out to accomplish something, there will definitely be challenges to overcome. Your challenges may come from different directions and in different forms than Nehemiah's challenges; but if you anticipate being challenged and are determined to remain focused, you won't be caught off guard when it happens.

Pause and Ponder

What challenges might you face on your journey toward the finish line?
How have you worked through challenges in the past?
What will keep you from working through your situation?
Who is spurring you on?

The people in Nehemiah's day battled discouragement. "The strength of the laborers is giving out, and there is so much rubble we cannot rebuild the wall" (Nehemiah 4:10). What has worked for you in the past to get beyond being discouraged when you know you are moving in the right direction?

ARTFUL LANGUAGE

In coaching conversations, we intentionally choose non-manipulative words that are free of any agenda.

Overcoming Challenges

The good news is, it is possible to break those challenging barriers. As an illustration, we would like to share a true story about an Olympic long-distance runner named Roger Bannister. Roger Bannister was a dedicated medical student who ran in the 1952 Olympics. Much to his dismay, Bannister, who was chosen to be the favorite to win the one-mile event, came in fourth at the '52 Olympics. Losing that race forced Bannister to make a decision about racing. He was at a crossroad and needed to decide if he wanted to stop running and stay focused on his medical studies or continue trying to break the four-minute mile.

With much encouragement from friends and family, Bannister decided to commit to breaking the four-minute mile while still pursuing his medical studies. On a windy, rainy day in Oxford, England on May 6, 1954, Bannister had another opportunity to run following his Olympic failure. The Daily Telegraph, at the time, described the sub-four minute mark as "sport's greatest goal," something "as elusive and seemingly unattainable as Everest."

Two fellow team members, Chris Chataway and Chris Brasher, would help set the pace. Chataway and Brasher had goals for each lap. Brasher started, hitting the mark on the first lap at fifty-seven point five seconds and Bannister was by his side. Chataway was the pacesetter on lap two and three—he and Bannister hit their marks of one minute fifty-eight point two seconds and three minutes point five seconds. Now, it was up to Bannister to finish the last lap. Tired, yet determined,

Roger Bannister broke the four-minute mile that day at three minutes fifty-nine point four seconds!

What an accomplishment. Bannister's perseverance and determination paid off. Interestingly, there is more to this story. It didn't stop there.

CREATING NEW AWARENESS

Discovering new ways of being and doing.

Within the next three years, sixteen other runners broke the four-minute barrier. Wow, that's amazing you say. The next sub-four minute time happened just forty-six days after Bannister's accomplishment. So, how was this possible? Was it because of improved training methods or better track shoes that so many runners were breaking the four-minute mile? No, the difference was in the mindset of the runners. Bannister erased the mental limiting beliefs and redefined what could be achieved.[2]

Pause and Ponder
What application can you make from this story?
Where will your four-minute mile race first be won?
What shift is necessary to give you traction and forward movement?

How does the idea of what "can't be done" or "can be done" impact you? For some, the obstacles and challenges could be the end of the story. Others, like Roger Bannister, are determined to overcome and keep on. These are the ones who know in their heart what they are to be doing and they remain strong. What will your response be?

Pride Must Go!

Both Nehemiah and Roger Bannister saw the importance of including others around them. Without a group of people to encourage them to cross the finish line, they may have never completed their goals. However, for both Nehemiah and Roger Bannister, they had to be completely honest about where they were— the fears they faced, the exhaustion they were experiencing, and the limiting beliefs that were holding them captive.

DIRECT COMMUNICATION

Being clear, concise, and laser-like with words.

What might be some things left undone in your process because you have not been totally open and honest yet? For many of us, one of the main deterrents God wants to break through in our lives during the Implementation Stage is pride. Pride says, "I don't need help; I can do it by myself." Pride also declares, "I don't want others to know what I really need." Pride is a personal challenge to overcome. If you need to do something about pride, let me encourage you to go for *it*, right now.

As we continue through the Implementation Stage, we will see the opposite of pride is humility; and out of humility, we will see the importance of becoming authentic.

Pause and Ponder

How might acknowledging pride help you to move forward in your process?

Perseverance Creates Authenticity

Perseverance and authenticity go hand in hand. Just like the process of creating authentic sea glass, an experienced coach has more than likely persevered through some of life's difficult times.

As coaches, we may have different backgrounds, different levels of education and training, and perhaps even different approaches to coaching. Although we are all unique by our color, size, and shape, most—if not all of us—have one thing in common, just like the sea glass, be it a common soda bottle to a piece of Depression glass, we have been tossed around in the waves of a disturbing sea of trials and buffed by the sands and pressures of life; which have transformed us into something unique and beautiful. Through perseverance, what was is no longer. We are constantly changing and hopefully for the better. That's what brings value to those who invite us to come alongside them on their journey.

Just to preface the next paragraph—in no way are we placing value on a person or a profession—we just want to share some fascinating facts about the value of authentic sea glass.

So, how can you tell if the sea glass is authentic? Well, the first clue is usually the price. Depending on how rare the color might be, the greater the cost. Did you know that orange sea glass is only found in one out of ten thousand pieces of sea glass? Second, what was the process in which the sea glass was polished? Did the glass go through all of the natural elements of rough seas, major storms, and deep, dark, and cold ocean waters or was the glass tumbled in a rock tumbler by some manufacturer of artificial sea glass? Only a master collector of sea glass can see the scars and depressions etched into authentic sea glass.

Likewise, it is important for us, as coaches, to be authentic and not take any shortcuts in the process. This does not mean you have to disclose everything in your personal life, but it does imply a sense of being present and real with those we coach.

THE COACHING RELATIONSHIP

Presence - a deeper level of knowing.

In his book, *The Coach Model for Christian Leaders*, Keith E. Webb says, "Don't be a coach, just coach. The word *coach* is both a noun and a verb. To be a coach (noun) is to have a position, role or title of coach. Just coach (verb) people! Listen well, be curious, ask questions about the other person's ideas before jumping in to share your own."[3] In other words, it is most important we create a safe place, an environment —like viewing a piece of art made from sea glass—that is inviting, calming, and peaceful.

Perseverance Gives Us Courage to Take the Next Step

In this chapter, we have been looking at perseverance during the Implementation Stage of the Nehemiah Response Coaching Model™. Often when we think of perseverance, our mind goes to stories of overcoming a catastrophic event, like our Hurricane Katrina experience, or a major obstacle, like breaking the four-minute mile for Roger Bannister. But what about those "mundane" situations that require us to persevere by just taking the next step?

- parents with a colicky newborn or a rebellious teen

- students deciding what to do after graduation

- couples going through a difficult time in their marriage

- a man or woman making a decision about a job change

The previous list is just a few examples of those who may be persevering on a daily basis, but their efforts go unnoticed. A mother standing watch over her feverish child throughout the night trying to decide what she needs to do will not make the morning headlines. Nor will many of the people we have mentioned be heralded as a modern day hero accomplishing the impossible; however, they continue to persevere in their daily lives.

Recently, we saw a perfect example of mundane perseverance. A young, injured bird was on the shoreline of the beach, and the waves from the Gulf were getting closer and closer to the injured bird. But then, we noticed a woman was standing next to the bird patiently waiting for the authorities to arrive to rescue the bird. At first, the woman's husband was standing alongside her; but then, he grew impatient and like others passing by, went on about his way down the beach. Vigilantly, she stood on the shore, watching the waves and waiting on animal control.

The fact is, this scenario was only one hour out of this lady's day, but she persevered. She remained steadfast, and when the authorities arrived, they allowed her to help with the rescue of the injured bird. How awesome is that?

So far in the Implementation Stage, we have seen the importance of taking action steps around the decision (plan) you have made, knowing there will be challenges, including our own pride. We also discovered that perseverance creates authenticity in our lives, and it takes courage to persevere no matter how large or small the challenge might be. In the next chapter, we will be focusing on the importance of serving, but first let us encourage you to take time to consider some or all the following questions:

Powerful Questions

When you feel misunderstood how are you affected?

What are the distractions that challenge you?

How do you stay focused and spurred on to move forward?

What keeps you from feeling overwhelmed when you have a big task to accomplish?

How does pride get in the way?

How determined are you to reach your goal?

POWERFUL QUESTIONS

Powerful questions promote the exploration of new possibilities and stimulate creativity.

Overcoming Challenges

7 serving others

I devoted myself to the work on this wall.
—Nehemiah 5:16

Nehemiah demonstrates servant leadership. He had now been appointed governor in the land of Judah. And instead of being like the governors who preceded him, he did not take advantage of his governorship and place a heavy burden on the people. Instead, during his Implementation Stage, Nehemiah worked alongside of the people and served others.

Our Response to Others

Why is it *the survival of the fittest* seems to be idealized? How might the Golden Rule be a better fit: "Do unto others as you would have others do unto you?" Jesus spoke the following words in his Sermon on the Mount: "Do not judge, or you too will be judged. For in the same way you judge others, you will be judged, and with the measure you use, it will be measured to you" (Matthew 7:1–2).

How much do we follow Christ's example of considering others? Sometimes, under pressure, we turn it around—doing unto others as they do unto us! In other places in the Bible, we read, "Love your neighbor as yourself." This was Jesus' response when he was asked about the most important commandment. In Matthew 22:37, 39, he replied, "Love the Lord your God with all your heart and with all your soul and with all your mind." Then Jesus said, "And the second is like it: 'Love your neighbor as yourself.'"

> Do nothing out of selfish ambition or vain conceit, but in humility consider others better than yourselves. Each of you should look not only to your own interest, but also to the interests of others. Your attitude should be the same as that of Christ Jesus. (Philippians 2:3–5)

We shared in chapter 1 the importance of understanding the other person's need by seeing the matter from their point of view. Well, consider a couple who is in the middle of a major crisis in their marriage. Both the husband and the wife will have a hard time focusing on the other person's needs because their own needs seem so much greater. Isn't it interesting though when each person takes the time to stop and really listen, not just hear what the other person is saying, but really listen; they are able to understand what the other person needs. By considering the needs of the other— not regarding what they need—their own needs end up being met, and the vicious cycle of self-centeredness is broken. What would happen if each person in the relationship would turn their "me" into a "we"?

DEEP LISTENING

The quality of our listening has bearing on the quality of our coaching.

Likewise, in chapter 5 of Nehemiah, we see some of the people were out for number 1—"me." They were in the mode of survival at any cost, even if that meant hurting someone. Why is it when we are overwhelmed with a task or we feel challenged, we act out in unusual ways? For some reason, many of us end up hurting others, and we act selfishly and demanding.

In their book, *Lead Like Jesus*, authors Ken Blanchard and Phil Hodges address this personal heart issue with the word ego as an acrostic—EGO.

They say, "As you consider the heart issues of leadership, a primary question you have to ask yourself is, 'Am I a servant leader or a self-serving leader?' The fact is we all fall short of perfection and give in to the temptation to behave as self-serving leaders in certain situations. The question, when answered with brutal honesty, reveals your motivation as a leader. It also reflects your heart's EGO: do you seek to Edge God Out or to Exalt God Only in the way you exert influences on those around you? The answer to that question reveals whether you are driven to protect and promote yourself or called to a higher purpose of service."[1]

Why is it we often hurt the ones we love? Why do we sometimes get irritated with those closest to us? The work of rebuilding for the people in Nehemiah's day was taking its toll. And like we saw in the previous chapter of Nehemiah, all of this internal friction came on the heels of what we've already seen. The people were becoming discouraged and tired. "The strength of the laborers is giving out, and there is so much rubble that we cannot rebuild the wall" (Nehemiah 4:10). And all of this came at an interesting point—when the work was half done. "We rebuilt the wall till all of it reached half its height" (Nehemiah 4:6). Fatigue had set in and what remained to be done was overshadowed by what had already been accomplished. They were discouraged, and their patience with each other had worn thin. So, as you can see, a reality check at the halfway point in any endeavor is critical.

It's Always Right to Do What is Right

As a servant leader, Nehemiah was a brave arbitrator desiring to do what was right (Nehemiah 5:9). The threat to slow down progress to rebuild the wall was

Serving Others

prevented by Nehemiah reconciling conflicts. When we are in the middle of our journey, "stuff" is going to happen. Doing what is right is always right.

Our objective is to keep moving forward. Be aware that forward motion causes friction. Conflicts are going to happen when you are trying to make progress and especially when you are under pressure. People may not fully understand what you are going through or they may feel you need to be approaching the matter in a different way. If this is the case, you will need to ask the Lord for wisdom as you seek out the best way to reconcile your differences.

The Goal—Reconciliation

During the Implementation Stage, it is essential to keep your team intact. Many theories of human interaction have been designed by sociologists. Bruce Tuckman introduced his theory called Tuckman's Stages in 1965. Most people recognize his theory by the names of the four phases of development: Forming, Storming, Norming, Performing. The goal of this process is to continue performing—working well together in a fluid way.[2]

In chapter 5, when the people were storming, Nehemiah worked toward reconciliation. Here is what happened: There were Jewish men who "raised a great outcry against their Jewish brothers" (Nehemiah 5:1). It seems in this case, money was the issue, and there were those who were taking advantage of the needs of others.

The first step Nehemiah took was to listen to both sides, "I pondered them in my mind" (Nehemiah 5:7). Then he declared to the lenders, "You are exacting usury from your own countrymen!" (Nehemiah 5:7). The next step, which can often be the hardest part in the reconciliation process, is getting both parties together and making things right.

The offender's final response to Nehemiah was, "We will give it back. And we will not demand anything more from them. We will do as you say" (Nehemiah 5:12). The reconciliation process is complete when the people involved in the situation: acknowledge their part, repent of wrong actions, seek forgiveness, and forgive the other person.

Being a Servant Leader

Here is where we look within and consider the kind of stuff we are really made of as a leader. Serving takes character, it's more about who you are rather than what you do.

Instantly, the inspirational story about Jim Elliot, a missionary to the Huaorani people of Ecuador, comes to mind. Jim Elliot was committed and had counted the cost of serving alongside four other missionaries in Ecuador in 1956. The mission, Operation Auca, was to reach and evangelize this particular people group. One day, while attempting to build trust among the people, the missionaries were brutally attacked and killed. Days before Jim Elliot was martyred, he wrote these words in his journal, "He is no fool who gives what he cannot keep to gain what he cannot lose."[3] That's servant leadership.

Pause and Ponder
How much does your vision matter to you? What are you willing to give up to reach the goal?
What changes need to happen to reach your goal?
How passionate are you about the vision God has placed in your heart?
How does your vision and "what can be" keep everyone motivated?

How we treat other people can be very telling about the kind of person we really are. At the end of chapter 5, Nehemiah shows us the kind of stuff he was made of. After he helped reconcile the two groups, he was promoted to governor. In verses 14 through 19 of chapter 5, we see that Nehemiah was a servant leader.

Let's take a glimpse of Nehemiah, the servant leader. Nehemiah said, "But the earlier governors—those preceding me—placed a heavy burden on the people" (Nehemiah 5:15). He never "lorded it over the people" (Nehemiah 5:15). "Instead, I devoted myself to the work on this wall," (Nehemiah 5:16). He served with no regard for money. And then, we see he was willing to serve others. He provided for the needs of over 150 workers out of his own pocket. That great number of people "ate at my table...Each day, one ox, six choice sheep, and some poultry were prepared" (Nehemiah 5:17–18). Nehemiah, "never demanded the food allotted to the governor, because the demands were heavy on these people" (Nehemiah 5:18).

It's interesting the same three marks found in the paragraph above about the servant leader, Nehemiah—not lording over the people, not greedy for money, and a willingness to serve others—are also found in 1 Peter 5:2–3. Actually, Peter lists the same three marks in reverse order. "Be shepherds of God's flock that is under your care, serving as overseers—not because you must, but because you are willing, as God wants you to be; not greedy for money—but eager to serve; not lording it over those entrusted to you, but being examples to the flock" (1 Peter 5:2–3).

Servant Leaders Are Change Agents

We know from the Scriptures we've been reading, Nehemiah desperately needed to repair the wall of Jerusalem and needed others to join him. In these final chapters, we see Nehemiah truly was a change agent.

So, what's the last success story you have heard about where someone, like Nehemiah, took charge and turned a near impossible situation around? Nehemiah turned his challenge into an unbelievable opportunity.

Pause and Ponder

What might be some ways for you to become a change agent? When is the last time you did something because it was the right thing to do?

The truth is, we may not be able to eradicate any of the issues we face in an instant; because the process of change can often be slow and challenging, and especially if you are working with a team. Getting and keeping your team genuinely on board is essential. Andrew Seidel, in *Charting a Bold Course* says,

> People will leave the status quo only when the pain of staying there is greater than the pain of leaving. The uncertainty and fear of the unknown is so great that people do not want to leave their comfort zone. They have to become convinced that remaining in the comfort zone of the present will somehow become uncomfortable. And they need to accept the discomfort of ambiguity as a natural part of transition. They have to believe that remaining in the status quo is far more expensive than the cost of transition.[4]

The good news is, as a coach, we have plenty of access to necessary tools to become a change agent. In his book, *Leadership Coaching*, Tony Stoltzfus says, "Simply stated, coaches are change experts who help leaders take responsibility for their lives and act to maximize their own potential."[5]

As a servant leader, we need to keep in touch with what God has in mind, join him, and put the tool belt of servanthood on, synch it up tightly, and use it effectively. We can all be change agents right where we are, right now.

Here are a few tools to consider adding to your toolbox to be a change agent:

1. Begin with a heart of gratitude for what you have (Colossians 3:15, 1 Thessalonians 5:18, Psalm 100:4)

2. Be observant, consider the needs of others (Philippians 2:3)

3. Serve wholeheartedly (Ephesians 6:7)

4. Be kind and compassionate. (Ephesians 4:32)

5. Take time to encourage others by building them up (1 Thessalonians 5:11)

In the next chapter, we want to address the topic of being a finisher. Often, it is easier to start a project than it is to see that project to completion. How can we be sure to finish?

Powerful Questions

What does the Golden Rule say to you?

What can you learn about yourself by the way you feel about others on your team?

What phase of development is your team in?

What help are they needing to move through a Storming Phase?

What about servant leadership can you apply to your own life?

Compare these passages and the three marks found of—not lording over the people, not greedy for money, and a willingness to serve others. (Nehemiah 5:14–19 and 1 Peter 5:2–3)

How hard is change for you?

POWERFUL QUESTIONS

Powerful questions promote the exploration of new possibilities and stimulate creativity.

8 finishing well

So the wall was completed—in fifty-two
days—this work had been done with the help
of our God.
—Nehemiah 6:15–16

Starting something is one thing; finishing is another! Finishing is especially important when it comes to working on a goal or working through a situation. So, to conclude the Implementation Stage of the Nehemiah Response Coaching Model™, we will look at the process of finishing.

You may be saying, "I know of some unfinished things that exist." For example, if you are a connoisseur of art, you may be familiar with the unfinished works of Michelangelo or perhaps you enjoy the intrigue of Franz Schubert's unfinished symphony. Both of these examples may be exceptions to the rule, however, normally finishing a project is essential.

It may be tempting, but let us encourage you not to take any shortcuts in your process. In the long run, it will be worth it to stick with the process and finish.

Finishing Is Challenging

When we read Nehemiah's story in the sixth chapter of Nehemiah, we learn he and the people finished their rebuilding project. "So the wall was completed...When all our enemies heard about this...they realized this work had been done with the help of our God" (Nehemiah 6:15). They finished, but it didn't come without the temptation of ending early or taking a shortcut.

When a project becomes overwhelming and we start to get tired, it's easy to convince ourselves that the job is done. We may begin to justify what we have done by saying, "This is good enough." Beware, you may find yourself being tempted to say, "Even though I'm not completely finished, things sure seem better than when I began all of this work."

This is exactly why the coaching agreement is so important. In the beginning of each session and throughout the process of ongoing sessions, the coach is there to check in with you and to encourage you to stay on track. It is so easy to lose momentum or want to shortcut the process. We often encourage people to be sure they feel confident before ending a relationship with their coach. Over the years, we have seen the benefit of finishing the process; so we want to encourage you to stay focused and finish.

THE COACHING AGREEMENT

Clarifying what the coachee wants to focus on.

Now, let's take a moment to look at the distractions that tempted Nehemiah to quit. Early on in chapter six, the enemies of Nehemiah began to come together to negotiate a plan of diversion. All of a sudden, people who were enemies were trying to befriend Nehemiah. They were saying, "Come, let us meet together in one of the villages" (Nehemiah 6:2). Something just didn't seem right to Nehemiah. Interestingly, as we continue reading the storyline, we discover Nehemiah's enemies came knocking on his door "four times" (Nehemiah 6:4) with the same friendly invitation, but Nehemiah didn't give in to the lure of something different or an offer for something that seemed better than what he was doing. Instead, Nehemiah realized the importance of finishing the job. He looked forward to the gratification and reward of knowing he and the other workers had finished the wall.

Be careful of the lure of something else before you finish what you are doing. Realize when things begin to change in your life, others will be affected but may resist change. There may be some people who are close to you that will not understand what you are trying to accomplish. They may even try to sabotage your progress and cause you to lose sight of your goal.

Finishing Takes Confidence

Finishing takes confidence and the will to never give up. It is so easy to get distracted, sidetracked, afraid, or consumed by counterproductive activities.

Pause and Ponder

How is finishing a challenge for you?
What causes you to get off task?
How do you handle diversion?
What does it take to have the confidence to never give up?

Paul was a finisher. In 2 Timothy 4:7, just before his death, he said, "I have fought the good fight, I have finished the race, I have kept the faith. Paul's secret to finishing may be discovered in another passage he wrote. Philippians 1:6, "Being confident of this, that he who began a good work in you will carry it on to completion until the day of Christ Jesus." Paul was a finisher because he knew God is a finisher! This is a compelling promise you can count on. *The Message* paraphrases Philippians 1:6 like this: "There has never been the slightest doubt in my mind that the God who started this great work in you would keep at it and bring it to a flourishing finish on the very day Christ Jesus appears."

In the movie, *Soul Surfer*, Bethany Hamilton's story inspires confidence to be a finisher. At thirteen, Bethany was attacked by a fourteen-foot tiger shark while surfing, causing her to lose her left arm. There were definitely difficult days; however, within six months, Bethany was surfing again competitively and winning, with one arm! She won the 2004 ESPY Award from ESPN for Best Comeback Athlete.[1]

Pause and Ponder

What do you have to finish?
What can be your next step in the right direction?
What goals have you set; but, have never finished?
From where does your confidence come?

Finishing Takes Courage

Recently, we were reminded of an incident that happened while Pam and our youngest daughter were in London. Pam was a rookie to the underground rail system, but our daughter was a more experienced traveler, so she was in charge of navigating the two of them through the web of the Underground.

One day, while on an adventure, they were in the Underground waiting on a train to come. It was extremely crowded on the platform that day, so our daughter said, "We are going to need to move quickly, if we are going to get on this train." As the train was approaching, people began pushing toward the edge of the platform. The train stopped, the doors opened, and the automated message came on, "mind the gap." The crowd began to pour out as those waiting on the platform began to work their way toward the doors of the train. Our daughter had finished the task of making it on to the train with the rush of people. Pam, however, was the next person to get on the train, when all of sudden, a man came out of nowhere—jumped in front of her and caused her to be pushed back further into the crowd. *Within that moment of hesitation, everything changed for her.* When she looked up across the gap between the platform and the train, she saw the doors of the train closing. There she was, standing on the platform, while our daughter was on the train.

As the doors began to close, our daughter realized her mom was not on the train with her. It was too late for Andrea to work her way through the crowd and out the doors before they would close. Unfortunately, Pam had completely missed the opportunity to be courageous to work her way through the crowd to get on the train. Pressing into the large glass window panes of the train car, our daughter could see the distress on Pam's face. When Pam saw our daughter, she cried out, Andrea, as she remained standing frozen on the platform.

The train slowly began to move down the track, and as Pam followed it on the platform, she could see our daughter trying to communicate something to her. Of course, Pam couldn't hear her, but she finally figured it out, "Get on the next train. I'll wait for you at the next stop." Such a simple solution and yet, Pam was overtaken by fear. Fear she was going to be separated from her daughter, and she didn't know how they would reconnect. Fear she was now alone. And, fear—that without Andrea—she could not navigate her way through the underground system. Fear of the unknown was powerful that day, and it paralyzed her to step over the gap.

Finishing Well

To this day, we laugh when we tell this story; but the day it happened, it wasn't so funny. Our daughter loves to tell people how she can still see the look of fear on her mother's face. She describes it, "As a mother who just watched her daughter be loaded up on a train to go to a refugee camp—separated forever." And, you know what? She's probably not too far off with that description.

Focused and Finishing

What keeps you from finishing what you start? Some may say, "It's just the way I am...it's part of my personality...I've always been like that." Or maybe you don't feel like you have the support you need to accomplish your dreams or goals, so you become discouraged and quit.

Whether it be yourself or others that keep you from completing a goal, how could you overcome the cycle of not staying focused and finishing? Here's a fitting Facebook post by the contemporary Christian author, Lysa Terkeurst. "Don't give up what you want long term, for what feels good short term. Avoid the terrible trade."

Well, talking about a terrible trade, here's a perfect example from nature. We have a bald spruce in our yard and the Cardinals love it. We can see the Cardinals flying in and out of that big, beautiful tree, hiding and building their nests. A few years ago, we decided to hang a bird feeder near the tree so the birds in our yard could have a bed and breakfast of sorts.

We had a Finch feeder and some seed in our garage, so we hung it up. Unfortunately, that only frustrated the Cardinals because they could not get the seeds from the smaller holes in the Finch feeder, so, instead, they would fly directly to the ground to eat the leftovers provided by the other birds.

After a few days, we decided to hang a bird feeder specifically for Cardinals. Well, do you know what those silly birds did? You guessed it, they kept going for the leftovers. But why?

If only you could have seen Pam standing in front of our kitchen window encouraging those Cardinals to "get their eyes on the prize." She would literally say out loud, "Come on...look up. Get focused...you just flew past the bird feeder. It's yours, go for it!"

Perhaps some of us are like those Cardinals. We can't believe that there is another option, so we quit or settle for something less. Or maybe we convince ourselves that we don't deserve anything better.

Finishing, it's an important part of the Implementation Stage. In this chapter, we have seen that finishing is challenging, finishing takes confidence, finishing takes courage, and we need to remain focused to finish. In the next chapter, we will look at the importance of celebrating.

Powerful Questions

How consistent are you at finishing a project?

What goals have you set in the past but have never finished?

What seems to get in the way?

What is your temptation to end early?

How hard is it for you to stay focused so you can finish a task?

POWERFUL QUESTIONS

Powerful questions promote the exploration of new possibilities and stimulate creativity.

PART 3

celebration stage

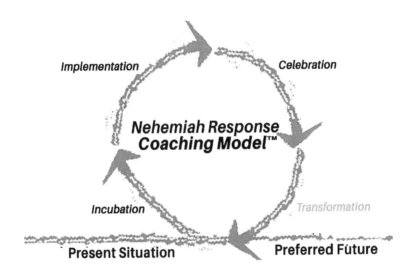

What is your tendency when you reach a goal? For many of us, we stop long enough to say, "Yay," and then we move on to the next project.

In the corporate world, we are hearing about venues where employees are actually rewarded with such things as casual Friday, game rooms, or even expensive getaways as a way to celebrate an accomplishment—be it a daily, weekly, or monthly goal.

However, it seems others are going through a

mundane routine in their lives, desiring to experience some kind of change to celebrate. What can you change? What can you celebrate?

The next stage of the Nehemiah Response Coaching Model™ is Celebration. Here's where we push the pause button for a while and savor the win—the little wins along the way and major wins as our coachee accomplishes a major project, has a life-changing breakthrough, or sees transformation in their life. Nehemiah 8:10 says, "The joy of the Lord is your strength."

How might you see this stage of the four stages being important to the people you coach?

Powerful Coaching Questions

Celebration Stage (see diagram)

- What is there to celebrate today?

- What is a good way to reward yourself because of your win?

9 time to celebrate

Go and enjoy choice food and sweet drinks...
the joy of the Lord is your strength. Then all
the people went away to eat and drink, to send
portions of food and to celebrate with great
joy... From the days of Joshua...the Israelites
had not celebrated it like this. And their joy
was very great.
—Nehemiah 8:10, 12, 17

Nehemiah led the way for a celebration following the completion of the wall. In chapters 7 and 8 of Nehemiah, we read where Nehemiah said, "After the wall had been rebuilt and I had set the doors in place, the gatekeepers and the singers and the Levites were appointed" (Nehemiah 7:1). They were getting ready for a celebration.

Likewise, as a coach, it is a good thing to stop and celebrate with the person, group, or team you are coaching on a regular basis. It is important to celebrate the little wins along the way, and it is always important to stop and celebrate the big wins. The third of the four stages of the Nehemiah Response Coaching Model™ is the Celebration Stage.

THE COACHING RELATIONSHIP

Presence - a deeper level of knowing.

Finishing Is Cause for Celebration

There was still work to do. There were houses that "had not yet been rebuilt" (Nehemiah 7:4). But there comes a time when you need to just stop and celebrate. In the eighth chapter of Nehemiah, we learn that "the people assembled as one man in the square" (Nehemiah 8:1). Then Ezra came on the scene, appearing for the first time in the book of Nehemiah. He was the priest, the spiritual leader who led the people into a time of celebration with singing, worshipping, and listening to the Word of God.

CREATING NEW AWARENESS

Discovering new ways of being and doing.

Although Ezra was in Jerusalem, he had not been mentioned up to this point. Actually, the work of rebuilding the wall of Jerusalem had overshadowed a time to worship; but now, the people were eager to worship and celebrate. In fact, this large assembly requested Ezra to "bring out the Book of the Law" (Nehemiah 8:1). Then, "He read it aloud from daybreak till noon...and the people listened attentively to the Book of the Law" (Nehemiah 8:3).

As a result of hearing the Word again, the people cried, and streams of tears flowed down their faces. The people were reconnecting with God again in an intimate way. The tears were expressions of sorrow because of areas in their lives, which did not line up with what they were hearing from the Word of God. Conviction had brought them to a point of change, and the end result was joy.

The people in Nehemiah's day were under conviction because something was missing in their lives. In their case, it was to observe a certain feast and "to live in booths during the feast of the seventh month" (Nehemiah 8:14). When they learned what was missing, they responded in obedience, and joy was restored in their lives. "From the days of Joshua son of Nun until that day, the Israelites had not celebrated it like this. And their joy was very great" (Nehemiah 8:17).

Pause and Ponder
Is there something missing in your life?
Has the work of reaching your goals diverted your attention away from spiritual things?

Nehemiah and all of Israel were full of joy and quite possibly overwhelmed with all the Lord had done for them. Now their tears were tears of joy and gratitude. At one point in their celebration, Nehemiah knew just what the people needed. He said, possibly with a big grin on his face, it's time to eat, "Go and enjoy choice food and sweet drinks...This day is sacred to our Lord. Do not grieve, for the joy of the Lord is your strength" (Nehemiah 8:10). And with those instructions, the entire crowd did just that—they "went away to eat and drink...to celebrate with great joy, because they now understood the words that had been made known to them" (Nehemiah 8:12).

Throughout this storyline, it is obvious the people were experiencing a new awareness. They were being awakened to the things they had been ignoring due to their busy lives. How might we as coaches, play an important role in creating a safe place where people can go deeper in order to experience new ways of being and doing things in their lives?

CREATING NEW AWARENESS

Discovering new ways of being and doing.

The same is true today, as it was in Nehemiah's day. There can be a realization that the goodness of God brings renewal into our lives. And here's something you can definitely take away from the Celebration Stage of the Nehemiah Response Coaching Model™— finishing is cause for celebration.

Celebration Comes Out of Sacrifice

When you hear the word celebration, what picture comes to your mind? Do you picture a festive event much like the people in Nehemiah's day? Whether it be a wedding, birthday, graduation, an anniversary, the birth of a baby, a ribbon cutting at an event, Christmas or Easter—all of these events call for a time of celebration; and just like for Nehemiah, no event comes without some kind of personal sacrifice.

In many of the events mentioned, the investment of time and money are vital; and in all of the events, dedication, perseverance, and a sense of commitment play a major role. Likewise, a whole gamut of emotions are usually experienced and expressed during a time of celebration. So, let us pose a question: "What is more significant, the process leading up to an event or the celebration itself?" In other words, "What brings you the greatest sense of satisfaction and pure joy?"

Ideally, we would all like to experience a time of celebration without sacrifice; however, Larry Crabb in his book Shattered Dreams states, "Happiness must be stripped away, forcibly, before joy can surface, before we will value and pursue dreams whose fulfillment produces true joy."[1]

And in James 1, we read,

> Consider it pure joy, my brothers (and sisters), whenever you face trials of many kinds, because you know that the testing of your faith develops perseverance. Let perseverance finish its work so that you

may be mature and complete, not lacking
anything. (James 1:2–4)

Celebration Comes Out of a Balanced Life

When our children were young, we took them to a
parade in a small rural town. In the not so far distance,
we could see a tractor coming down the street. What
drew our attention to the tractor was not all of the
clowns around the tractor, but the fact that the tractor
was going up and down as the driver tried desperately
to keep the tractor in the center of the street. At a
closer glance, we realized someone had welded the
axle off center on each of the wheel frames to cause the
tractor tires to be off center. When we see something
like this in a parade, we laugh, but in real life, it's not so
funny.

In this illustration of the unbalanced tractor,
someone had *intentionally* welded the axle off center
on the wheels of the tractor to cause it to be
unbalanced. Are you like the tractor in the parade,
struggling to stay balanced or are you choosing to live
an *intentional* life that is well balanced? So, how do you
stay balanced?

Unfortunately, most of us rarely take the time to pause, breathe, and think about what's working well in our lives. Maybe you are saying, "There is just too much to do and not enough time to do it...let alone *pause to listen, reflect, and maintain balance in my life.*"

Pause to Listen:

1. Stop what you are doing and take the time to listen to God, to trusted friends, to a coach or mentor.

2. Find a quiet place where you can spend uninterrupted time alone to pray, meditate, and listen.

3. Be prepared to listen to your body. What are you doing to improve your health?

4. Listen to how you respond to situations and others by keeping your emotions in check.

5. Intentionally choose not to let circumstances get the best of you.

Reflect on what influences you:

1. How do I respond to those in my circle of influence—family, friends, neighbors, coworkers?

2. What or who challenges me to be a better person? How willing am I to make the changes I need to make in my life?

3. How am I growing in a deeper understanding of my own physical needs, emotional needs, and spiritual needs?

4. How am I spending time reaching out to others?

Remain balanced:

It takes a conscientious effort to remain balanced in your life. You must choose to bring yourself back to the center; and every time you do, you will find more balance and proper rhythm in your life.

The Joy of Celebration Energizes

Well, as we close this chapter, know this one thing—God is okay with a time of celebration. Romans 14:17 reads, "For the kingdom of God is...righteousness, and peace, and joy in the Holy Spirit." In Galatians 5:22, we learn about the fruit of the Spirit which is "love, joy, peace, patience, kindness, goodness, faithfulness, gentleness and self-control." Psalm 19:8 tells us, "The precepts of the Lord are right, giving joy to the heart."

God endorses celebration. So go ahead, give yourself permission to celebrate something good that has happened. Celebration is a time to experience the joy of all you have accomplished. It's also an opportunity to break away from all of the doing and to be refreshed. Once you have experienced a time of celebration, you may want to incorporate regular times of celebration into your life. In the book titled, Rhythm of Life, author Richard Exley expresses how vital celebration is for balance in our lives,

> Another equally important, but less recognized discipline is the rhythm of life —that delicate balance between work and rest, worship and play. Meaningful work gives our lives definition and purpose. Yet, without a corresponding amount of rest, even creative or spiritual work becomes tedious...Worship and play must then be added to the work/rest cycle to produce the Abundant Life.[2]

Nehemiah 12:27, Jerusalem celebrated "joyfully the dedication with songs of thanksgiving and with music of cymbals, harps, and lyres."

As we have seen in this chapter, celebration brings about reflection which energizes us. Reflection also gives us an opportunity to respond to God with change in our lives. Plus, celebration really does energize us and prepares us for moving out again as we will see in the story about a Coastal pastor Nelson has been coaching. Nelson was sitting with a pastor in his office for a coaching session, when the pastor began to open up about being exhausted. He said, "My weariness is causing me to become frustrated with people and ministry; both of which I love. I don't like feeling this way."

And so, this pastor and Nelson set out on a coaching journey, and in the process, the two men became friends. They laughed and cried together. And in time, the pastor began to smile more; and Nelson could hear a renewed energy in his voice. One day, at a session, the pastor began to describe his coaching experience. He said, "Nelson, I'm glad for Katrina, because if it wasn't for that devastating storm, there wouldn't be a Relevant Ministry and the coaching you provide to pastors along the Coast. We lived and worked fifteen minutes from each other before Katrina, but we were each in our own 'silos' at the time, doing our own thing. Gratefully, we're not only out of our 'silos'; but, you are sitting here in my office celebrating with me. Thanks for being my coach and helping me gain a 'second wind' to keep moving forward. It's renewed my love for my people and church where I serve."

Just like this pastor who experienced joy and a renewed energy to move forward in his ministry again, it is time to determine the kind of person we want to be in the days ahead. The next chapter will help us see the importance of becoming the kind of person we need to be as we look at the fourth and final stage in the Nehemiah Response Coaching Model™—the Transformation Stage.

Powerful Questions

How good are you at taking time to celebrate?

What steps could you take to stop the cycle of going from one project to another?

What might the integration of celebration into your life mean?

What sacrifices have you made to be able to celebrate?

How satisfied are you with balance in your life?

POWERFUL QUESTIONS

Powerful questions promote the exploration of new possibilities and stimulate creativity.

PART 4

transformation stage

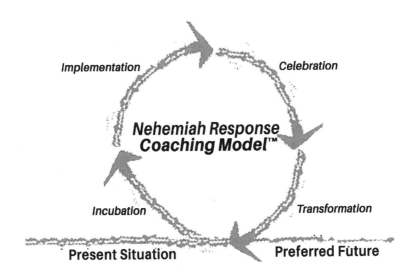

The fourth and final stage of the Nehemiah Response Coaching Model™ is Transformation.

The goal has been reached, what now? You have worked hard. How has your experience changed you?

When the people in the book of Nehemiah finished the wall, they didn't sit down. They were impacted by how their experience and accomplishments had changed them.

We believe our friend, Jamie Aten, did a great job summarizing the Nehemiah Response Coaching Model™, highlighting the Transformation Stage.

> Nelson's Nehemiah Response Coaching Model™ is a "how-to" biblical transition process. The model, integrated with social and behavioral sciences, fits well with the Transtheoretical Model which proposes how we change. What I like about the Nehemiah Response Coaching Model™ is that it goes beyond behavior change to transformation.
>
> —Jamie D. Aten, PhD
> Founder and Co-director,
> Humanitarian Disaster Institute
> Department of Psychology
> at Wheaton College

In the next and final chapter, we will explain the Transformation Stage.

Powerful Coaching Questions

Transformation Stage (see diagram)
- How do you see God working in your life?
- What are some new insights?
- How have you been changed?

10 a transformed life

In view of all this, we are making a binding
agreement, putting it in writing, and our
leaders, our Levites and our priests are affixing
their seals to it.
—Nehemiah 9:38

When they finished the wall, the workers didn't sit down at the finish line; instead, the Scripture tells us they had a major response. "In view of all this," they saw their accomplishment of rebuilding the wall as a partnership with God, and their response was one of personal transformation. The Transformation Stage is the fourth and final stage of the Nehemiah Response Coaching Model™.

Responses to God's Blessings

"Day after day, from the first day to the last...they celebrated" (Nehemiah 8:18). Being energized from their celebration, the people who had rebuilt the wall were now ready to move on to what was next. We discover in chapters nine and ten of Nehemiah the people began to spend some time reflecting on the kind of person they wanted to become. They realized God had done so much for them, so what was their response to be in return?

They prayed and sought God for the answer. Their seeking was so intense the Bible says they "gathered together, fasting, and wearing sackcloth and having dust on their heads" (Nehemiah 9:1). You might say they were serious about seeking God for what was next in their lives!

In the two months it took them to rebuild the wall, they had experienced God in incredible ways. They had experienced his power, his provision, and his protection. The rebuilding led to renewal and celebration, and they wanted more. However, their desire for more wasn't about selfish ambitions; they had figured out what life is all about. They were ready for a deeper commitment and change. They'd risen above the physical realm where we so often spend our time. They had experienced God in a whole new spiritual way!

Pause and Ponder

How are you partnering with God in your process?
What is your response to God because of His blessings?
What is your level of commitment for change in your life?

In Nehemiah chapters 9 and 10, the people review their history in a public gathering. It was a time of counting their blessings. Then we find them making some important promises about things they had come to realize as essential in rising to the spiritual plane where they desired to be. Their spiritual renewal led them to spiritual awakening—revival in the purest sense of the word; it was as if they were truly living again.

In reviewing their history, they were reminded of the goodness of God over the years. They were riveted with the reality of how awesome God is by saying, "You are the Lord God" (Nehemiah 9:7). "You have kept your promise because you are righteous" (Nehemiah 9:8). "You sent miraculous signs" (Nehemiah 9:10). "You divided the sea" (Nehemiah 9:11). "You came down to Mount Sinai" (Nehemiah 9:13). "You are a forgiving God, gracious and compassionate; slow to anger and abounding in love" (Nehemiah 9:17).

They had arrived at an important place of decision-making. They were ready to commit to be fully devoted followers of God. Because they realized, beyond a shadow of a doubt, God was committed to them, they were beginning to grasp the importance of mirroring that same level of commitment back to him by saying, "God, who keeps his covenant of love" (Nehemiah 9:32).

Do you remember Nehemiah's first prayer in chapter 1, verse 5, "O Lord, God of heaven, the great and awesome God, who keeps his covenant of love."? Here's the exciting thing—the people had come full circle with the reality of God's faithfulness and their encounter with God brought about their transformation.

It may yet seem impossible to believe, particularly depending on where you are in your process, but your situation can lead you to a deeper place of spiritual living. When you follow God's example of commitment, God keeps his commitment of love to us—the question is, what is our commitment to him?

Pause and Ponder

When is the last time you considered the goodness of God in your life?
How can you mirror God's commitment to you back to him?
What is something you should be changing in your life to be a transformed person?

These thoughts regarding transformation bring us to a story about the storm-destroyed trees after Hurricane Katrina. Not long after Katrina, chain saw artist began showing up all along the Coast creating beautiful pieces of art out of the destroyed live oak trees. All along Beach Boulevard you still can see dolphins, cranes, pelicans, fish, turtles, and other forms of coastal life artists created out of the trees. It was amazing what an artist could see inside of the tree—his vision for how to transform a dead tree into something which brought back life. It took the storm and the destruction of the tree for the artist to cut away and reveal what was inside; transforming the tree into something beautiful.

　　　　　　A Transformed Life

It's the same for each of us as we keep growing as disciples, committed followers of Jesus Christ—something beautiful happens as we let God change and transform us.

- Biblical transformation is the process of death and rebirth where our weakness becomes strength for His glory.

- Transformation means life change of the believer by the intentional choice to no longer "conform to the pattern of this world, but be transformed by the renewing of your mind." (Romans 12:2)

- The outcome of being transformed is a life that reflects the likeness of Christ. "Being transformed into his image with ever-increasing glory." (2 Corinthians 3:18)

Pause and Ponder

How are you being challenged to be transformed today?
What barriers stand in your way?
Who can help you?
What will you do next?

Our commitment to how we will respond to God's blessings and how we intend to live our lives is how we express our love back to God. It is like a couple in a marriage ceremony expressing their love and commitment to each other with their marriage vows. In John 14:15, Jesus said, "If you love me, you will obey what I command."

What was it the people of Israel committed to after their rebuilding? How can we promise these same commitments to God right now in our lives? As disciples of Jesus Christ, what can we commit to today?

Growing–Going–Gathering–Generosity

Let us share with you an alliterated outline of what is found next in this passage of Nehemiah with these words: growing, going, gathering, and generosity. These four words represent responses to God for his blessings to us and can be spiritual practices to add to our lives as followers.

ACTION AND ACCOUNTABILITY

Brainstorming, designing the action, and follow through.

The first word is *growing*. They "separated themselves..." (Nehemiah 10:28). The Jewish people were to be a distinct people to their world. For followers of Christ, separation from the world is expressed in our dedication to God. Dedication is all about *growing*. Paul commented about the believers in

Thessalonica saying, "You turned to God from idols to serve the living and true God" (1 Thessalonians 1:9). And in Romans 12:1–2, we read,

> Therefore, I urge you, brothers, in view of God's mercy, to offer your bodies as living sacrifices, holy and pleasing to God—this is your spiritual act of worship. Do not conform any longer to the pattern of this world, but be transformed by the renewing of your mind.

What is God saying to you about dedication to him and *growing*?

Then the people made a commitment "to obey carefully all the commands, regulations and decrees of the Lord our Lord" (Nehemiah 10:29). This step of obedience represents an action response—*going*. It's one thing to know what we need to do, but to do it is another thing. In the New Testament, James 2:17 says, "In the same way, faith by itself, if it is not accompanied by action, is dead."

How can your commitment to God be expressed by action, obedience, and the word *going*?

Gathering is next, and Nehemiah 10:31 is about honoring the Sabbath. Today, gathering happens any time believers get together. Other words are community and fellowship—it's all about belonging.

"And let us consider how we may spur one another on toward love and good deeds. Let us not give up meeting together, as some are in the habit of doing, but let us encourage one another—and all the more as you see the day approaching." (Hebrews 10:24–25)

What's your habit for *gathering* with other believers?

The final word is *generosity*. In Nehemiah, "The people...are to bring their contributions of grain, new wine and oil to the storerooms" (Nehemiah 10:39). We see the early church in the New Testament practicing *generosity*. Even to the extent of, "selling their possessions and belongings and distributing the proceeds to all, as any had need" (Acts 2:45). *Generosity* is about all of these—our treasure, our talent, and our time.

How satisfied are you with your practice of *generosity*?

These four words are spiritual practices we can carry out as a follower of Jesus Christ. These practices, though, are not what transform us; by practicing them, we make room for a deeper relationship with God.

By *growing, going, gathering*, and *generosity*, Christ is revealed in us through our transformed lives.

Commitment Requires Change

Making such commitments requires change. Change can be hard and maybe that's why we so often find ourselves breaking commitments. What can we learn about change? Have you ever traded for a newer car after driving one for a number of years? Were all the controls in different places? If so, how long did you keep turning on the wipers when you wanted to set the cruise control? Habits are hard to change. In the same way, we can get too comfortable with where we are in our relationship with God.

Granted, some things should not change. "Stand at the crossroads and look; ask for the ancient paths, ask where the good way is, and walk in it, and you will find rest for your souls" (Jeremiah 6:16). In the New Testament, Paul said, "Hold firmly to the trustworthy message as it has been taught" (Titus 1:9).

Some things don't change; however, there are things that should change—and that change starts with us. "Therefore, if anyone is in Christ, he is a new creation; the old has gone, the new has come!" (2 Corinthians 5:17).

Pause and Ponder
What kind of person will you be now?
What might be your first step?
How committed are you to taking the steps to live
a transformed life?

The transformation from where you once were to where you are now can be seen in the metamorphosis of a caterpillar to a butterfly. Now, it's time to spread your wings and fly, what can you learn from the people in Nehemiah's day?

ARTFUL LANGUAGE

In coaching conversations, we intentionally choose words that are non-manipulative and free of any agenda.

1. When they arrived at their goal, they took time to count their blessings.

2. They realized they had gotten to where they were because of God's commitment to them, and they chose in return to commit to him.

3. They were willing to make changes and develop new disciplines in their lives.

This may be the last chapter in the book; however, this chapter will continue to be written as lives are transformed through the coaching process. As we wrap up, we would like to leave you with a testimony from a coachee,

> I am very pleased with the coaching process. Through self-discovery, I have overcome some very large hurdles on my journey. I believe the coaching process is transforming and I wish everyone could experience the invigorating power it possesses.

As a coachee or as a coach, what will your level of commitment be to a life long journey of living a transformed life?

Powerful questions:

Review the four Gs in the chapter. What notes can you make about how God is speaking to you?

Growing:

Going:

Gathering:

Generosity:

How challenging is change for you?

If change is hard for you, why do you think that is?

What are some evidences of your transformed life?

POWERFUL QUESTIONS

Powerful questions promote the exploration of new possibilities and stimulate creativity.

notes

Part I

Incubation Stage

1. J. Val Hastings, *The Next Great Awakening: How to Empower God's People with a Coach Approach to Ministry*, 15.

Chapter 1 Being Centered

1. http://coachfederation.org/need/landing.cfm?ItemNumber=978&navItemNumber=567
2. Steve Ogne and Tim Roehl, *Transformissional Coaching: Empowering Leaders in a Changing Ministry World*. 10–21.
3. Gary R. Collins, *Christian Coaching: Helping Others Turn Potential into Reality*. 16.
4. Robert E. Logan and Gary B. Reinecke, *Coaching 101 Handbook: Discover the Power of Coaching*.

Chapter 2 Having a Vision

1. George Barna, *The Power of Vision: Discover and Apply God's Plan for Your Life and Ministry.* 30.

2. Will Mancini, *Church Unique: How Missional Leaders Cast Vision, Capture Culture, and Create Movement,* 167.

3. Andy Stanley, *Visioneering: God's Blueprint for Developing and Maintaining Vision,* 18.

Chapter 3 Developing a Plan

1. Richard J. Foster, *Freedom of Simplicity,* 91.

Chapter 4 Abiding in Faith

1. Nelson Roth, *Nehemiah Response: How To Make It Through Your Crisis,* 58–59.

2. E. H. Hamilton, *Afraid? Of What? And Other Poems And Sketches,* 7.

3. J. Val Hastings, *Accelerated Coach Training,* 75.

4. Ibid., 76.

5. The *Wheel of Life* concept was originally created by Paul J. Meyer, founder of Success Motivation Institute, Inc. www.mindtools.com/pages/article/newHTE_93.htm

Part II

Chapter 5 Starting Strong

1. Russell Conwell, www.britanica.com/topic/Acres-of-Diamonds.

Chapter 6 Overcoming Challenges

1. Linda J. Miller and Chad W. Hall, *Coaching for Christian Leaders: A Practical Guide*, 37.
2. https://en.wikipedia.org/wiki/Roger_Bannister
3. Keith E. Webb, *The COACH Model for Christian Leaders: Powerful Leadership Skills for Solving Problems, Reaching Goals, and Developing Others*, 153.

Chapter 7 Serving Others

1. Ken Blanchard and Phil Hodges, *Lead Like Jesus*, 40–42.
2. https://en.wikipedia.org/wiki/Tuckman%27s_stages_of_group_development
3. Elisabeth Elliot, *Shadow Almighty: The Life and Testament of Jim Elliot*.
4. Andrew Seidel, *Charting a Bold Course, Training Leaders for the 21st Century Ministry*, 220.
5. Tony Stoltzfus, *Leadership Coaching: The Disciplines, Skills, and Heart of a Christian Coach*, 6.

Chapter 8 Finishing Well

1. http://abcnews.go.com/Primetime/Health/story?id=644247&page=1

Part III

bibliography

Books:

Barna, George. *The Power of Vision: How You Can Capture and Apply God's Vision for Your Ministry.* Regal Books, 1992.

Blanchard, Ken, and Phil Hodges. *Lead Like Jesus: Lessons from the Greatest Leadership Role Model of All Time.* W Publishing Group, 2005.

Conwell, Russell. www.britanica.com/topic/Acres-of-Diamonds.

Collins, Gary. *Christian Coaching: Helping Others Turn Potential into Reality.* Navpress, 2001.

Exley, Richard. *The Rhythm of Life.* Honor Books, 1987.

Foster, Richard J. *Freedom of Simplicity.* Harper & Row, 1981.

Hamilton, E. H. *Afraid? Of What? And Other Poems And Sketches.* 1960.

Hastings, J. Val. *The Next Great Awakening, How to Empower God's People with a Coach Approach to Ministry.* Coaching4Clergy, 2010.

Hastings, J. Val. *Accelerated Coach Training: Coaching4Clergy Textbook.* 2011.

Logan, Robert and Reinecke, Gary. *Coaching 101 Handbook: Discover the Power of Coaching.* Churchsmart Resources, 2003.

Mancini, Will. *Church Unique: How Missional Leaders Cast Vision, Capture Culture, and Create Movement.* Jossey-Bass, 2008.

Miller, Linda, and Chad Hall. *Coaching for Christian Leaders: A Practical Guide.* Chalice Press, 2007.

Ogne, Steve, and Tim Roehl. *Transformissional Coaching: Empowering Leaders in a Changing Ministry World.* Nashville: B & H, 2008.

Roth, Nelson. *Nehemiah Response: How to Make It Through Your Crisis.* Tate Publishing, 2009.

Seidel, Andrew. *Charting a Bold Course: Training Leaders for 21st Century Ministry.* Moody Publishers, 2003.

Bibliography

Stanley, Andy. *Visioneering: God's Blueprint for Developing and Maintaining Vision.* Multnomah Books, 1999.

Stoltzfus, Tony. *Leadership Coaching: The Disciplines, Skills, and Heart of a Christian Coach.* 2005.

Webb, Keith. *The COACH Model for Christian Leaders: Powerful Leadership Skills for Solving Problems, Reaching Goals, and Developing Others.* 2012.

Websites:

www.coachfederation.org
www.coaching4clergy.org
www.relevantministry.org/coaching

index

The 8 Building Blocks of Coaching[1]
Find them in this book in these chapters: